High Hopes

High Hopes

Taking the Purple to Pasadena

Gary Barnett with Vahé Gregorian

WARNER BOOKS

A Time Warner Company

Warner Books, Inc., 1271 Avenue of the
Americas, New York, New York 10020

W A Time Warner Company

Printed in the United States of America

First Printing: September 1996

10 9 8 7 6 5 4 3 2 1

ISBN: 0-446-52099-3
LC: 96-60602

High Hopes was produced by
Bishop Books of New York City.

I would like to dedicate this book to my father, Leland Barnett. "If it's worth doing, it's worth doing right," has become a part of my very being. His love of sports, his competitiveness, and his passion for his family has been missed for some 16 years now.

My only wish is that he could have shared this season with me, my family, my team, and my mother.

Acknowledgments

The authors are grateful to Rocky Walther, Visions Sports Management's Mike Ward and Mark Dunn, and Warner's Larry Kirshbaum and Rick Wolff for the engineering of this project. The final product would not have been possible without the technical assistance and encouragement of the *St. Louis Post-Dispatch*'s Jim Mosley and Jeff Goedelman, and the staff of Bishop Books, in particular senior editor Carrie Chase.

Also instrumental were Northwestern football program coordinator Jeff Genyk; Northwestern sports information director Brad Hurlbut, and Lisa Juscik and Mark Simpson of his staff; and Sherry Herget, Judie Kleecamp, and Brenda Trapp of Walther-Glenn Law Associates.

Thanks to Steve Musseau, Robert Neuschel, *Post-Dispatch* sports editor Mike Smith, and Warner's Rob McMahon, Tina Andreadis, and Julie Saltman.

—Gary Barnett and Vahé Gregorian

Contents

Preface

There is magic in the way Gary affects people.

As I look back on the beginning of our relationship, I still remember being intrigued. I was sharing a seat in sophomore P.E. class with a tall, attractive, muscular young man with fantastic forearms. This was the same guy who had been a stout, annoying jokester with dark horn-rimmed glasses the year before. After this initial meeting, Gary asked me to help him collect coins for the March of Dimes. I accepted his invitation and the course of my life changed completely. I was, and continue to be, completely enamored with Gary. Little did I know then what was in store for us.

Over the 28 years of our marriage, I have come to appreciate what an extraordinary communicator Gary is. He has a special way of motivating and encouraging people (myself included) to find the inner strength, will, and determination to succeed. With this confidence comes the ability to accomplish great things.

Gary has the uncanny ability to teach complex ideas through the use of concrete and visual stories. A gifted storyteller, he creates an inspiring and motivating vision that everyone can take home. I have been on many a mission to find the perfect magic water pitcher or scientific scale (complete with beans and nuts) to illustrate his points. Players, coaches, and just about anyone can draw from Gary's philosophical lessons and insights to achieve and exceed their goals. Sometimes I take Gary's gift for granted, yet it is amazing to see how he can ignite a spark and help others achieve far more than they ever imagined.

Of course, Gary is incredibly competitive. Living with him can be looked at as a series of challenges. When we are both driving separately to the same destination, we will have a contest to see who arrives first. These are among the contests I am likely to win, simply because Gary spends most of his driving time en route to the office or airport, unaware of my shortcuts. I have learned that most situations provide a challenge, and Gary loves a challenge.

From my point of view, Gary's strongest coaching attribute is his genuine care and concern for the football family—the players, coaches, and their families. Somehow, Gary communicates to everyone involved that they are a critical link in the chain necessary to build a successful football program. The coaches' wives are genuinely appreciated for all the contributions they make to the program—from bringing players home-baked goodies to manning the canned food drive or hosting recruiting events. As demanding and time-consuming as this profession is, it is exciting when the team families collectively help *move* the band wagon.

Gary's nature makes him quite vulnerable. He regularly blames himself for most things that go wrong, many of which he has no control over. He is incredibly hard on himself, yet I find this an endearing quality—frustrating, but endearing. As a father, Gary has high expectations and can be tough with our children—yet he is really quite gentle. He has a great sense of humor and always seems to have the perfect one-liner or story to ease any friction or tension. He always has just the right words to make us all feel better and realize that our problems are simply *unsolved possibilities*. We are both very proud of our children: Courtney and Clay are our greatest achievement.

The coaching life is intense. Its cyclic nature delivers a new phase just when change is drastically needed. Recruiting, spring ball, summer camps, the regular season, bowl games, and then the anticipation of starting all over again. I guess Gary, the ceaseless planner, is fortunate to have found his opposite—we are a good balance. He has encouraged me to be my own person, and in turn, I have helped support and push him toward his goals.

I wouldn't change a thing. However, in all honesty, with the success we have had with the Big Ten championship, I must admit that I am having a little difficulty sharing my husband with all the people and well-wishers who want a piece of his time. But if that is my only complaint, things must be going pretty well.

I am extremely happy for Gary and the success he's had, and I know, like everything in our life together, this is just the beginning—a stage in a progressive process. I am excited and ready to push my way through the next series of challenges. I am proud of the ethics and relationships Gary has built over the years and his reputation as a coach. What Gary has done is one of those rare examples of how sheer determination and passion, coupled with a great staff and extraordinary kids, can truly—and collectively—bring about amazing results.

—Mary Barnett, June 1, 1996

Introduction

In the abyss between Northwestern University's Rose Bowl seasons, in its stupefying 46-season futility dance, the toothless Wildcats became the chewtoy of the Big Ten Conference, a trifle to be alternately gouged and pawed at.

Between 1971, when it last achieved a winning season, and 1995, Northwestern mustered a mere 46 victories in 253 games and in the process came up 4,649 points shy of its foes. In one particularly appalling span, dubbed "The Tranquil Period" by Northwestern insiders, the school lost 34 successive games and went five years without a Big Ten victory.

The school's humiliation reached a crescendo in 1981, when Northwestern went 0–11 in gaudy style. The combined score for the season: Opponents 505, Wildcats 82.

Even Northwestern's 1949 cameo appearance in Pasadena was largely a contrivance: The Wildcats had finished as runners-up in the Big Ten that season but were beckoned west for New Year's Day because of a no-repeat rule prohibiting conference champion Michigan from accepting the berth.

Northwestern last had enjoyed football prosperity around the turn of the century—when its typical schedule featured the likes of Englewood High School, Transylvania, Chicago Physician & Surgeon and Municipal Pier—and had won at least a share of four Big Ten titles from 1926–36.

In the modern era, though, the prestigious institution amassed titles in more cerebral pursuits, such as a record eight National Debate Tournament championships. On the football field, the only consistent rebuttals to the weekly beatings came from the sparsely filled stands at Dyche Stadium, in Evanston, Illinois, where a generation of students consoled themselves with chants of, "That's alright, that's okay, you're going to work for us someday."

1

Scuttlebutt persisted that Northwestern, the only private school in the Big Ten, would de-emphasize the sport—insert your own punchline here—and attempt to join the Ivy League.

In the 10th game of the 1992 season, Gary Barnett's first as coach, Iowa hammered Northwestern 56–14. After the game, Iowa coach Hayden Fry approached Barnett and said, "Hope we didn't hurt any of your boys."

—Vahé Gregorian, June 1, 1996

Part One:

Belief Without Evidence

1.

Expect Victory

"Failure is not an option."
—from the Universal Studios movie **Apollo 13**

When it comes to Northwestern football, most people who weren't paying close attention might have thought of a different quote from that movie. Like, "Houston, we have a problem." After all, we had gone 8-24-1 in my first three seasons, beginning in 1992. You couldn't blame the uninformed for thinking the program still was going nowhere fast.

What they didn't understand was that at 211 degrees, water is just hot. At 212, one more degree of temperature, water turns to steam, which can create enough energy to move a train through a mountain pass. We were simmering at 211.

In the spring of 1995, I firmly believed we were on the precipice of something special. I'm not going to say I knew we would lead the nation in scoring defense—but I knew we would have a healthy, rugged Big Ten Conference–worthy defense. I can't say I knew we would go to the Rose Bowl—but I knew we were ready to win games.

I thought we might be a year from maturing and blossoming, but during the Big Ten preseason media luncheon I said, "We're ready to make a move in this league." When I was asked who I thought would win the conference, I smiled but wasn't exactly joking when I said Northwestern. People reacted like I had been smoking weed.

But everything was unmistakably building and brewing in the spring. You could just sense it. When we finished spring practice, I held up a picture of a Velociraptor from the movie *Jurassic Park*. I told our guys, "This is what happened this spring: A baby Velociraptor has just broken through its egg.

"We have three months to grow up," I said, pointing to this nasty picture, "and become this."

For someone not intimately involved, it would have been hard to have a sense of where we were. I gained a real appreciation of this in the spring of 1996, when I was the color commentator for SportsChannel's broadcast of our spring game. As I sat up in the booth and watched, the first thing I thought was, "No wonder broadcasters and sportswriters can be so critical."

Up there, insulated behind the glass, far from the field, they can see the game but they can never feel it. On the sideline, you feel it—the speed, the struggles, the pain, the noises, the strategies, the smells, the accomplishment of making even a first down. The beauty and all the remarkable aspects of football, more than any other game, come from being immersed in the environment.

If you're not down in there, well, you're just watching plays unfold. So when I take the local beat writers out to dinner before this season—something I do every year—I may challenge them to spend some time with us on the sideline this year.

During the first three years at Northwestern, coaching was like learning to drive a stickshift. You had to consciously hit all the pedals, shift the levers, hit the accelerator, steer. Every movement was conscious and labored. At some point in 1995, Northwestern football turned into a smooth-shifting automatic.

All I had to do was point the team in the right direction and provide a little acceleration now and then. Even then, most of the time I could put it on cruise control. There was so much positive energy in the group that I just had to rev it up, let it go and keep out of the way.

To me, beating Notre Dame in our first game required no quantum leap—even if on the way back from South Bend, Indiana, I experienced one of the most intense feelings I've ever had. I sat there on the bus grinning like I had physically given birth to my first child. I remembered when my wife, Mary, had our boy, Clay. She stayed up all night smiling, and now I sort of knew how that must have felt. Sort of.

Those of us in the eye of it all just felt like what we were doing was right. We were taking the necessary steps and doing what we as coaches had decided were the right things to do in all these situations. It seemed to lead to a logical, sequential outcome, and the truth is any program can do what we did. Many, many times along the way it was hard to feel like we were making any progress, but those who could be close to it all yet step away enough to be objective could see something shaping.

The discipline of not falling off the road you've chosen is

essential, but the guidelines we came to use are actually pretty basic. They're simple concepts for success that you don't necessarily need a football coach's affirmation to make special.

We always approached our goals with more than just the football field in mind, because we didn't want to be about winning at all costs. The true satisfaction for us was going to be in turning the team around and knowing we had done it properly and fairly, without compromising our values or priorities.

No matter what somebody does in his or her particular walk of life, there are issues of right and wrong to make decisions about. It's usually harder to do the right thing and honor your conviction. What the right things for us at Northwestern were always seemed obvious. They had to do with belief and trust and patience. Caring. Listening. Having faith. Extreme hard work. Hunger.

Those might sound trite, but that's only because too many people talk about those qualities without understanding them or taking them to heart. To overcome our many obstacles, each of those qualities had to be there. They were all part of the puzzle, and we had to focus keenly to know how to integrate them all.

A picture that comes to mind is this: When you walk across stones in a stream, you must concentrate on the stones—because the minute you look up to see what's passing by, you're going to slide in the water. You have to focus on the stones and precisely where your feet are going.

That kind of focus comes naturally for me, though I have to admit it's not necessarily always a virtue. I probably inherit the stick-to-it-iveness from my mother, Edith, and in me it's almost obsessive. Even when things probably need to be stopped, I can't let go until they're absolutely finished.

For example, when I get up on a Sunday, there might be three or four things I've decided I have to do. It might not be anything important, just stuff like running or watching part of a golf tournament or going over to the office to look at a film. But if I don't find some way to do all four or five of those, I almost turn into a jerk—don't I, Mary?

If I've decided on a flight plan, that's it. I'm on the flight plan, and you can't get me off it. It doesn't need to be that way. I mean, at times it's ridiculous at home. But it's probably okay at work.

I'm an extension of my mother in other ways, too: Every single person is important to her, and they are to me, too. That's why when I meet people I work hard at remembering their names. I say to myself that a person's first name is one of the most important things they have, and I know how valuable it is to be able to say, "Hey, Hudhaifa," instead of, "Hey, how you doing?"

That feeling probably is also why I always thank people for asking me for my autograph. I consider it an honor to be asked. I always will.

Even if I wasn't totally surprised by the good that came on the field in 1995, I won't pretend I was remotely prepared for the sideshow that followed.

The steadily growing attention from the public and the media, I had gotten used to. But from the minute Michigan beat Ohio State to leave us the undisputed Big Ten champion and launch us into the Rose Bowl, our world spun out of control. In fact, everything began to change in the middle of that game.

When it looked like Michigan might win, strangers cascaded into our football building, the Nicolet Center, where we were watching the game in the auditorium. Hundreds of people were there by the end, blowing horns, waving flags and hollering.

Roses were everywhere, although the Rose Bowl people kind of messed up by not being there to personally present us with the bid. They did it by camera. Just for the fun of it, I didn't accept right away. I said I needed to ask our players whether they might be interested. It turned out they were.

Had we gone to the Citrus Bowl, which was where we were heading if the Rose Bowl hadn't worked out, I'm not sure the ensuing publicity would have been what it was. Once we got the Rose Bowl bid, everything just kicked up into turbo. Everything tripled in magnitude: I'm talking media, fans, everything.

One day, the voice mail and E-mail systems at the university just blew up because they were so overloaded with congratulations and ticket requests. Hundreds of letters came in almost every day, from Italy, Switzerland, all over this country.

I tried to give a handwritten response to each one—every time I got on a plane I'd write notes—but I've still got a couple of stacks waiting to be answered. Hopefully I haven't offended anybody.

It all reached a speed and excitement level that I had never experienced before, not even when I was an assistant coach at Colorado and we won the national championship. I didn't know it could be that way. I don't think I understood how important the Rose Bowl was.

Mary and I got home that first night and there were roses all over our front porch. People had just stopped by and left single roses. Many came from people we didn't even know. Around Evanston, people hung big Northwestern flags in front of their houses and drove around the streets with Northwestern banners on their cars. I hadn't seen any of that before.

At stores downtown, there were actually lines of people to buy Northwestern gear—and they were selling out. The Locker Room, a store across from Dyche Stadium, got phone calls requesting bumper stickers from as far away as Singapore and Morocco.

It was hard for me to fathom the interest we generated. It seemed like someone from every facet of society contacted us at one point or another.

House Minority Leader Richard Gephardt called from my home state of Missouri. He's a Northwestern graduate. I called him back and said, "Dick, how you doing?"

He said, "Congratulations. You know, we Democrats have been getting our butts kicked in Congress. We need to maybe have you and [our voluntary motivational coach] Steve Musseau come in here and talk to us. We need to believe again."

I said, "Okay," but I still hadn't heard back from him as of mid-May.

Our feat even reached various houses of worship. After the Rose Bowl, I got a letter from another Northwestern grad, the Rev. Richard B. McCafferty of Livermore, California.

"Two weeks ago you were compared to John the Baptist in a homily delivered at all three of our Masses," he wrote. "Let me explain: One of our regular preachers is a Dominican nun, Sister Rebecca Shinas. Central to her homily was John the Baptist, the herald of Jesus Christ. She commented on the TV closeup of you (in the Rose Bowl) as your kicker hit the left goalpost as the game wound down. You had a wry smile on your face, more resigned than angry.

"Sister's point was that it was obvious that you felt much more sorrow for your kicker than for the loss; as John the Baptist was always thinking of not himself but the person who would come after him and was far greater than he.... You have wrought a miracle, not quite on the level of the loaves and the fishes but certainly comparable to David downing Goliath."

Obviously, I'm a little uneasy about such comparisons and remarks, but it did become clear to me that we had captured the

9

hearts of America. That's what I said when Ann-Margret—another Northwestern alum—presented me with the "ESPY," ESPN's award for coach of the year.

Even if at times I felt awkward about the way people were viewing us, I have to admit we managed to have a lot of fun with the situation.

I mean, Wheaties featured Northwestern football helmets on its cover. It wasn't exactly the same as your childhood dream of having your face on a Wheaties box, but it was close. Pretty close.

Minnie Mouse gave me a smooch at Disneyland. At our pep rally in Pasadena, so many actors who were alumni of Northwestern showed up that it seemed like a Broadway show. Hollywood took notice, too. In one interview I had talked about how much the movie *City Slickers* had meant to me. There's a scene where Curly, played by Jack Palance, holds up his finger and says, "You know what the secret of life is? This. One thing. You stick to that, and everything else don't mean ..."

I almost came out of my chair when he did that. It was a defining moment for me: The way you live your life is the secret to life. And you do one thing, you stick with it and do it absolutely well.

The thing was, in the interview I then called *City Slickers* this "dumb movie." A week later, I got an overnight package from Billy Crystal, who directed the movie and played the character Mitch. He wrote:

"Dear Coach Barnett:

"I've been following your football team with great interest. My daughter is a graduate of Northwestern during the good ol' days of ineptitude when the football team was terrible but the math team was unbelievable.

"I read an article where you quote a scene from *City Slickers*. I'm glad that it affected you in a great way. But then imagine my surprise when you then referred to it as a 'dumb movie.' Coach, I am very proud of the film. I am sure you didn't mean it as it was printed, but these stories get picked up and those words take on a life of their own. So, Coach, next time you refer to *City Slickers* (which I hope you do), please don't call it dumb. I would really appreciate that.

"Best of luck in your march to a bowl game. I really am a fan and thank you for getting people to forget the Lombardi years of the Northwestern math team."

He signed it, "Kindest personal regards" and even included an autographed script of *City Slickers*.

Charlton Heston, an alum who had written me a note of encouragement during the season, on our behalf returned to his role as Moses in *The Ten Commandments* and parted a Purple Sea for us at Universal Studios. As he did it, he said, "Behold the power of the Lord! The very waters shall honor thee, turning to our school colors, purple and white."

When we were in California, we also got to go on *The Tonight Show with Jay Leno*. When I had been running earlier that week, I came up with an idea to get a huge, long chin strap for Jay. Bill Jarvis, our equipment manager, put it together.

Leno was wonderful. He made you feel so comfortable, it was easy to do the show. He is a legitimately funny guy, and he is so humble. He's overcome a lot of adversity, and I can see how he's done it. He's got a spirit about him that's almost contagious.

The whole team was there for the show, and they were excited since the other guests included Gena Lee Nolin from *Baywatch* and Donna Summer, the singer. When I sat down, I told Jay, "You know, one of the things that happens after our games is that all of the young kids want our players to give them their chin straps. It's a nice memento."

Then I pulled out the giant chin strap and said, "I know after your last game back at, I think, Andover, you gave some lad your chin strap. We talked that young man into giving it back." Jay didn't know I was going to do this, and he really got a kick out of it.

That night probably was the highlight of our trip. The kids had so much energy, and Leno showed the film clip of the skit they had done with Charlton Heston. The idea was that the team had been stranded because of a flood, so we couldn't get to the Rose Bowl. As it turned out, there was a real irony to using that image.

Among the pre-Rose Bowl traditions is the "Beef Bowl" at Lawry's, where players from each team compete to see who can eat the most meat. I believe our guys ate 673 pounds of beef, so we beat USC by about 70 pounds. I think we could have had another 150 pounds, but Lawry's cut us off. We had some guys lumbering around a bit after that, but at least we won that competition.

Some neat things happened in the months afterward, too. Growing up in Mexico, Missouri, I'd listen to the St. Louis Cardinals game every night on KXEO. That's what you did. We didn't have television, but even if we did we would have listened to the Cardinals.

Harry Caray and Jack Buck did the games every night, and every night I'd lie there and drift to sleep and my dad, Leland, would come in and turn the radio off. Baseball probably was my favorite sport. So when I was asked to throw out the first pitch at Wrigley Field to open the 1996 baseball season, well, the Rose Bowl topped everything but this had to be second.

I remember seeing President Clinton throw a high, arcing, slow pitch when he tossed out an opening day pitch once, and I didn't want to embarrass myself by doing that. I actually practiced for about four days. But when it came to the moment of truth, I didn't get to warm up any at Wrigley. My pitch was a little off the mark, but at least I threw it hard.

Then I got to go up to the press box and sing "Take Me Out to the Ballgame" with Harry Caray. It was incredible, even if I did sing the wrong words and got razzed about it on the radio later.

Seventeen national coach of the year awards came in for me, and there was another from *Playboy* that I declined to accept. I don't want to sound holier-than-thou, but I just thought it was the right thing to do considering my family.

One of the particularly interesting awards I got was the one given by the Downtown Athletic Club of Glenwood, Iowa. The superintendent of schools, a shop teacher, the chief of police, and a banker there started it up a year ago, in a coffee shop. They came to town for a Chicago Bulls game and brought the trophy over to my office. The trophy is beautiful—it even has a map on it showing where Glenwood is.

But probably the two awards that made the greatest impact on me were the ones that actually went to the entire staff: the American Football Coaches Association Award, voted on by my peers, and the Bobby Dodd Award.

My feeling was, and I said this, that I got to win those awards with 10 of my best friends. You know that the reason you win any of these awards is that everybody else did a great job. In my case, it was my staff—and the people who touch our kids directly: academic support, trainers, weight-room people, equipment managers....

All the fuss that was made about the season naturally changed our daily lives. Mary and I couldn't go into restaurants anymore without hearing people whispering my name and staring and coming up to congratulate us. Before when people recognized me, it was along the lines of, "Poor baby." Now it was like, "You get to do that?!"

At Chicago's O'Hare Field, I was having to get security escorts because I'd get stopped so frequently. It wasn't that I didn't want to talk to people, but I was almost missing flights and if I didn't get help I was going to have to offend someone or walk away from someone.

Often it's flattering to be recognized, but there are times you'd just as soon be anonymous. For example, back in Evanston shortly after the Rose Bowl, somebody drove by me on the road and flipped me off. I had no idea why. I drove maybe another 200 yards then said, "Man, this is bull. I don't have to take that."

I turned around and followed the guy probably three miles, then I got stuck at a light. I saw where he was going, though, and my heart was pounding while I was waiting. The light turned green, and I jumped out ahead of everybody and turned into the parking lot. There he was.

He had parked his car, and he was getting out. I screeched my tires, pulled up behind him and got out. I said, "Excuse me!" He turned around, and he was about 65 years old.

"What did I do to deserve to get flipped off?" I said.

He said, "Hey, aren't you the Northwestern football coach?"

"Wait a minute," I said. "That's beside the point. What did I do to deserve to be flipped off?"

"What do you mean, flipped off?"

"You gave me the finger."

He looked at my car and said, "No, no, I gave it to the car behind you. I gave it to a green car that was giving me trouble."

Then he said, "Hey, can I have your autograph?"

I gave him the autograph, thanked him for asking, then got back in the car and drove off.

2.

Chaos

"The remarkable thing is we have a choice
every day regarding the attitude we will embrace for
that day. We cannot change our past. We cannot
change the inevitable. The only thing we can do is play on
the one string we have, and that is our attitude.
I am convinced that life is 10% what happens to me and
90% how I react to it. And so it is with you. We
are in charge of our attitudes."
—*Charles Swindoll*

People ask me what it's like to coach football at Northwestern. The best example I can give is by contrast.

When I was an assistant coach at Colorado in the 1989 season, we played for the national championship in the 1990 Orange Bowl against Notre Dame. We lost, and it was a bitter disappointment.

By the time we got back to the hotel, it was 1 A.M. and we had an early plane the next morning. At about four in the morning, there was a disturbance out in the hallway and I got up to see what was going on. Two of our players were out there high-fiving, low-fiving—celebrating.

"Men," I said, "what is going on here? We just lost the biggest game of our careers, and you're out here celebrating?"

They said, "Coach, you've got to understand. We just finished putting together a jigsaw puzzle!"

I said, "Jigsaw puzzle? When did you start it?" They told me they started in August. "August?" I said. "This is January."

They said, "Yeah, but that's what's so exciting—on the cover it says the jigsaw puzzle is supposed to be for two to four years."

Okay, that's a joke, so I hope nobody takes offense. But it is a tad different coaching at Northwestern than at most other schools.

After all, with the exception of Stanford, we have the highest average standardized test scores in major-college football.

I remember when we were at Colorado and struggling to get over the hump, trying to get our kids to understand what it was to play hard. Bill McCartney, the head coach and one of the most influential people in my life, stood up in front of the team one day and said, "We are going to perform a metamorphosis. Do you know what metamorphosis means?"

No one raised a hand. And he said, "It's change that's caused by heat, pressure and time." It was a vivid, clear analogy, and I thought his delivery made a powerful impression.

So in his first defensive team meeting here at Northwestern, our defensive coordinator, Ron Vanderlinden, started out, "Guys, we're going to undergo a metamorphosis. Does anybody know what a metamorphosis is?"

About eight guys raised their hands: "Coach," somebody said, "it's change, caused by heat, pressure and time."

Vandy just got this look of shock on his face. That took a little drama out of what he was trying to say, but he collected himself quickly and kept on going: "Well, that's right! It's heat and pressure over time, and that's what's going to happen with this football team."

On our flight to Stanford in 1992, Mary and I were sitting behind Ryan Padgett, who was a freshman offensive lineman. He had headphones on, and Mary asked what he was listening to. Ryan said, "Classical music." Mary's heart sort of fluttered.

She said, "What are you reading, Ryan?" He was reading Shakespeare. Then he got up after our meal and Mary asked, "Where you going, Ryan?" He said, "To brush my teeth."

Mary couldn't believe it. She said, "Oh my God: He listens to classical music, reads Shakespeare and brushes his teeth after every meal. I want him to marry my daughter. This can't be a football player."

Of course, a lot of people had just that image of Northwestern football players—and thought it appropriate considering there hadn't been a winning season here since 1971 and the school had only won as many as four games twice in that time. In our football media guide under the category of "Selected Northwestern Firsts and Facts," the last real mention of football on the time line is 1949—when Northwestern beat California in the Rose Bowl.

When you think about the great traditions of college football, then, maybe it was only fitting that Northwestern's was students tossing marshmallows at each other and the band. After all, they didn't have anything else to do.

The students also seemed to have a thing about tearing down goalposts. I try to avoid dwelling on the negatives of the past, but I heard somewhere that they even tore down the goalposts after some record-setting loss and chanted, "We're the worst!"

What was important to me wasn't what had happened or why but that it be changed. All I cared about was understanding where we were so we could get to where we wanted to be. As much as I didn't want to know about the past, though, the fallout was impossible to ignore.

They used academics as an excuse for our poor athletic performance here, but the truth is the academics should have been a boost for athletics—not an obstruction. But they had to have some excuse, or how could anyone condone what had been going on? People acted like if you could write or speak, that meant you had some congenital condition preventing you from being able to run.

I don't like the converse of that view, either: the assumption that because we had success in football last season we must have forsaken our standards. Like our defensive tackle Matt Rice once said: "We're no dumber now than when we stunk."

The reality is that this had become a slothful football program that people distanced themselves from. It was so embarrassing, I guess the only way alumni or people on campus could deal with it was to ridicule it or disassociate from it. Certainly, no one wanted to risk the emotional or financial commitment to try to change it.

Soon after I took the job—and probably a little before I took it—I found out that everybody around the program shrank back from the thought of truly investing themselves in it. Everybody thought small; the first answer to everything we wanted to try was automatically, "No," instead of, "Let's find a way to do it."

This was the basic environment I walked into, and this is where the jigsaw puzzle comes in.

People think that there's one or two or three things that you do to make a change or a difference in a negative environment, or that there's some type of master blueprint you can draw up and use as a guide. Frankly, I don't think there's any one thing I can put my finger on. But the closest analogy I have for our situation is a jigsaw puzzle.

When you buy a jigsaw puzzle, the only way you know what

that puzzle is supposed to look like is by looking at the picture on the top of the box, the vision of what the puzzle should ultimately be. But when you open the box, the first thing you see is chaos.

What a jigsaw puzzle represents, though, is a system for turning chaos into order. That's what we set out to do, just like we used to do on our card table at home when I was growing up.

Before we could do anything else, we had to figure out precisely what the cover—our vision—was going to be. At the first staff meeting, I said, "If you can't see the invisible, you can't do the impossible." Invisible and impossible as it might have seemed, what I saw was the Rose Bowl.

At our basketball arena later that night, January 11, 1992, I was introduced to our student body. When I was handed the microphone, I blurted out, "We're going to take the Purple to Pasadena"—to the Rose Bowl. The students all went nuts, and as I left the court I sort of wished I hadn't said it. But once I made that statement, which came from a sentiment of former Northwestern player John Yale, it became the top of the jigsaw puzzle. We had committed ourselves to that vision.

When I make a commitment it's like what Cortez did when he conquered Mexico. He left no way out for his men—he burned the boats. There was no turning back; there was only the rest of Mexico. Now there was no turning back at Northwestern. When I made that statement, I burned the boats. Every decision from then on was going to be based on whether it would ultimately get us to the Rose Bowl.

We immediately got a Rose Bowl banner and hung it in the entryway to the Nicolet Center. I put a 1949 Rose Bowl ticket on display on one of my desks. I got a Rose Bowl poster from 1949 and put that up. My high school baseball coach, Don Sparks, had sent me a nylon rose that I put in a bowl in my office. We staggered our recruiting mailings with pieces of a jigsaw puzzle that came together with a picture of the Rose Bowl.

We had a very, very clear idea of where we were going to go. At least in our minds. Emotionally, there would be many times I doubted we could ever get it done. Intellectually, I always believed we would. I guess you could say I'm an idealist. That's why I took this job.

It was like I told Coach McCartney one time: The way I see people is they're like vines in a window box. When you first put a vine in a window box, the box is huge and the vine is small. But eventually, if you give it space and nurturing and freedom, that vine will grow into that window box and fill it up. And then you'll need a bigger window box.

That's what opportunities are: a chance to grow until you need a bigger box. To me at this job, I was a small vine in this huge window box. The only limits on me were the size of the box that I put myself in. And that's why I wasn't afraid when someone would say, "He's never done this before," or "This is going to be totally new to him."

Before we actually began rummaging through the box, I thought it was important that we as a coaching staff establish an approach that would serve as a guiding light in assembling the jigsaw. We had to decide what we were about first.

Our philosophy was: 1) Coaching was about taking people where they couldn't take themselves; 2) Every player deserved a coach who believed in him; and 3) Winning was about getting everybody to play with one heartbeat.

Early on, we also created two Mission Statements that we now print in our media guide, which also is used for recruiting.

"Our mission is to take the student-athlete where he cannot take himself. We will foster an environment that teaches young men to:

"1. Relentlessly pursue and win THE BIG TEN CHAMPI-ONSHIP!

"2. Appreciate and embrace cultural diversity.

"3. Achieve an exemplary foundation of leadership and academic success."

"Our mission is based on the values of family, successful attitudes, and team chemistry.

"We believe in honesty, integrity, strength of character, care, and confidence.

"We embrace a commitment to excellence, loyalty, selflessness, trust, and humility.

"We teach overcoming adversity, establishing priorities, goal setting, and the value of diversity."

As we looked deeper in the jigsaw box and reached in to begin clustering pieces by color, we found some pieces were missing. A lot of pieces didn't fit or were damaged. So we had to craft the pieces we needed, some of which couldn't be worked on right away.

For instance, because of recruiting restrictions, we could basically only change 20% of the team each year. It would be five recruiting classes—five years—until we would be coaching exclusively our own players. That's not to slight those we inherited but to say that we had no immediate control of personnel—among other matters.

I can't even begin to describe how much we couldn't control. An example is the "police escort" we got for our first home game.

From our hotel, our bus was stopped at every stop sign. We stopped at every red light. In fact, as we were coming down one street the policeman stopped us to let traffic go through! Local drivers had more right of way than we did with a police escort. I was sitting on the bus, steaming, and the kids were looking at me like, "We're pretty big-time here, huh?"

Finally, I couldn't take it any more. I ran out and told the escort this wasn't exactly what I'd had in mind and said, "Don't you know we're going to a game?" I probably sprinkled a few rude words in there, too.

He said, "You get your ass back on the bus, or you're never getting to the game." I dropped my head and walked back onto the bus.

So we had to begin by trying to reach and influence that which was within our power and scope. We could only craft what we could grasp, and that started with assembling the border of the jigsaw puzzle and then addressing individual parts.

I looked at five things, in no particular order, that I thought would create its border.

One imperative was to create an atmosphere of trust and respect. The great game of football teaches that we need each other. When you're one of the 11 guys with your hands locked in the huddle, it doesn't matter whether you're white or black, Democrat or Republican, rich or poor. All that matters is being able to count on your teammate.

I made a mistake in the trust process early on. I assumed because there were so many years of losing here that everybody was anxious for a change. Not true.

I had taken the place of Coach Francis Peay, a former teammate of mine at Missouri and, at the time he was fired, one of two black head coaches in Division I football. When I walked in, I thought that the 69 players I inherited were excited. What I did not take into account was that most of the kids, especially our 35 black kids, had come because of Francis Peay.

20

They came to Northwestern because he was such a tremendous role model, and because he was a strong black man. And then all of a sudden, he's yanked away from them—yanked especially hard from the freshmen, who had only spent three months with him. They were in some ways very angry and reluctant to accept a new guy.

I also assumed that Northwestern had been operating much like the other Big Ten schools. Wrong. We were vastly behind in all operational senses, including budgets and seemingly minor matters like mandatory study halls and workout sessions.

It took going through an entire season before I fully realized how behind we were, particularly in terms of the kids' approach. They just had never been made to do the things that we coaches considered obligatory, and when I came in and demanded it of them, they had nothing like this in their history ... and who is this guy, anyway?

I was a stranger. I hadn't met their parents, as I would have had I recruited them, and there was no bond between us. If I had it to do over again—or if I ever do this again—during Christmas break I would have gone into the home of every athlete that I inherited and sat down with the young man and his parents and explained my expectations. I would create relationships.

Without having done that, though, we still groped for ways to reach our players. In my office, I put up a sign that said, "This meeting may only be interrupted by a player." I wanted to make sure that they knew they were the most important people here, that I wanted them to come up into our offices and that no matter what we were doing, we would drop it to talk to them. They should never feel as though they were interrupting anything.

We began eating dinner with the players, and they acted like that hadn't happened before. We went into the locker room with them after practice and hung out, and they acted like that hadn't happened before. I remember one of the players walked into our offices upstairs, and he said, "Hi," to the secretary, Dolores Morrison. I said, "Dolores, do you know who this is?" She said, "I have no idea," and the guy had been there four years. So I made the secretaries cut the players' pictures out and learn their names.

While I wanted to acknowledge the individuality of the players, they had to understand we were foremost a family. They needed to know that the family is what's most important and that there was no room for special privileges. That also meant understanding the need for discipline, which I consider something you do *for* someone and not *to* someone. Regardless of each person-

21

ality and how it may resist discipline, I believe players really are crying out for it.

Among the points I needed to learn, though, was that "family" was something different from what I had experienced. Where I came from, when my dad said "Jump," I said, "How high?" That wasn't necessarily the experience our players had had at home.

At least a third of our kids came from single-parent families and now had to answer to male authority more than they ever had before, some for the first time. If we couldn't grasp that, there was going to be a constant irritant between players and coaches.

The second border of the puzzle we had to construct was to create an atmosphere where football was important, because football was not important on campus. It wasn't important within the university, and it had come to a point where it wasn't even important to some players.

We started a picture board downstairs of prominent alumni. We put up our goals, so they could be tangible. We put up Northwestern football pictures all over our offices, which had had nothing on the walls, and we set up a spring alumni game to bring people back into the program.

I would go to campus "firesides," where our faculty and staff meet with students, and talk about what our program was going to be about. I found that our students, just like the ones at Michigan or Wisconsin or Illinois, wanted to have something to get excited about on the weekends. It wasn't that they didn't appreciate or enjoy sports or want to be a part of athletic excellence. It was that they couldn't find it and were frustrated.

Another thing we did to breed a sense of significance was to take a week of summer practice off-campus. We're on a quarter system at Northwestern, which means that when the players report for camp in early August there is still more than a month until classes begin. With all the potential distractions of Evanston and Chicago, we didn't think having them stay here the entire time was conducive to focused training.

Tim Kish, one of our assistant coaches, found two potential sites in Wisconsin, where the Chicago Bears go for camp in the "Cheese League." The first, St. John's Military School, was absolutely perfect: a spartan old school with iron beds. But it was too far away and would have been a logistical nightmare.

Then we looked at the campus of the University of Wisconsin-Parkside in Kenosha. It was a little posh for what I wanted, but it ended up being ideal. It was out away from everything, but it still was only about 45 minutes from campus.

The off-campus practice sessions gave us credibility, I think, and helped to communicate football's importance. Not only had Northwestern never done it before, but it's my understanding that nobody in the Big Ten had, either. Kenosha became a special place.

While the coaches have a great deal of influence, all the other people who come into contact with your kids day-to-day can also have a tremendous effect. In a football program—and, I imagine, in any organization—you have to be absolutely aware of who influences your people, your players. They need to be able to breathe and drink a winning attitude from every possible outlet.

So we had to make sure that our academic support people, our medical people and our weight-training staff were thinking the same way we were thinking; they often would be around our players at their most vulnerable moments. They had to share the same vision on the jigsaw puzzle box.

Initially, they didn't. How could they? Nobody on campus other than the coaching staff had ever been around a winning football program—or an important football program. Ever.

The third border was to establish systems. Offense, defense, terminology, schedules, operations and just the way things work. It sounds dull, but it's essential. I don't see how any entity can function, let alone thrive, without clear delineation of responsibilities, priorities and tasks.

I knew our greatest immediate problem would be defense, so we had to set up our offense to control the ball and help our defense. There are two ways to do that: You can either run an option attack and bore everybody to death, or you can have a short passing game and try to dink everybody to death.

As I looked at our personnel in 1992, none of the quarterbacks we had were really option quarterbacks and it was too late to recruit one. That meant it would be at least three years before we could have a suitably experienced option quarterback, and I didn't feel like we could be that patient. So we decided on the short-passing game.

Instilling a work ethic was a fourth border of the puzzle. When I met with the team for the first time, I told the players I wanted them to ask more of themselves than they had ever asked before.

But they had to ask it of themselves. If I had to ask it of them, it wouldn't mean as much. It needed to come from an intrinsic feeling, not from outside prodding.

In football, the most important factors in how good somebody can be lie in the heart and the decisions that are made about commitment.

Obviously, there has to be a certain minimum level of physical ability. But after that, I believe the potential for achievement is virtually unlimited. If you have the same physical credentials as the guy you're playing against, or the guy who performs at a high level, then the only thing that keeps you from performing at that level is you.

This is accountability. You put it back on the players. They need to understand that the only reason they're not as good as someone else is because they choose not to be as good. We're going to provide you with all the things you need to be physically as good, I tell them, so if you don't measure up with your opponent or the All-American it must be because of a decision you made or something inside of you.

There is a story about a boy who goes to the zoo and sees a man selling balloons. The man has some helium balloons and some regular balloons. The kid sees a red balloon slip away from the man, and it goes straight up in the sky. Then the guy lets go of a green balloon, and it just sort of falls to the ground and bounces around.

So the kid says, "Mister, I want a red balloon." And the man says, "Why a red one?"

"Because it's the one that goes up in the sky," the boy says.

The man says, "No, no, it's not the color of the balloon; it's what's inside the balloon."

It might be easy for us to see that, but it's also up to us to help our guys understand that—and to help them accordingly with their choices. I have to show them that every time they make a poor choice, whether it's in conduct, academics or work ethic, that this is a choice leading them away from being as good as they can be.

Sometimes we had to make vigorous demonstrations to get their understanding. I remember going to an early study table once, to see if all the guys were there. Maybe a third of them weren't.

I said, "Where's Chuck Robinson?" Somebody said, "Probably still in bed." So I got the keys from his roommate and went to his dorm room. There he was, sleeping in. I pulled the covers back, pulled Chuck out of bed and said, "Get your butt down to study table."

He was shocked, of course. But you had to do those sorts of things to establish standards.

The final border was the recruiting of talent.

We had a real deficit there, and the phrase I use all the time—which came true again at this year's Kentucky Derby—is, "I have yet to see a jockey carry a race horse across the finish line."

We inherited, I believe, only two players who had been invited and taken recruiting visits to other Big Ten schools. We had a receiver who was 5'3". Our lack of speed was a liability. Some of our guys, remember, had been recruited off an 0–11 season in 1989.

So we had to launch a major talent search. There were and are so many selling points for Northwestern, from arguably the most valuable diploma in Division I football to our beach on Lake Michigan to accessibility to Chicago. There was no reason for us to be shy about going after the same kids Notre Dame and Michigan were going after.

The history of the program might have been an impediment for some, but here's how I approached that:

With almost every player I've visited at home, at least until this year, I have asked if they have ever made anything with their hands. Maybe it was in shop class, or art class, or somewhere else.

Most of them have done it, of course. So I'd ask them to show it to me. It might be a birdhouse, or it might be a stool or it might be an ashtray. I'd say, "You know, you could buy one of these at the store." They all go, "Sure." And I'd ask, "But which one means more to you? The piece that you made—or a piece that you bought?" Every one of them says the piece that they made.

Well, I'd tell them, coming to Northwestern would be a lot like that, because you have a chance to build something. You have a chance to do what nobody else has ever done. You have a chance to dig the foundation, do the masonry work, put in the mortar, put up the walls.

Now, you can go to other places where the walls are already up, and the buildings are already there and you can just sort of get to rent. You're just another guy. But if you build a house or rent a house, which one do you have more ownership in? Which one do you have more pride in? That's what I used as an appeal.

Unfortunately, initially, a lot of guys said they'd rather rent.

Making matters worse, our first year we weren't tremendously familiar with the parameters for admission. Probably 60% of the applications we sent to admissions for pre-approval—which a prospect needs before he can even make an official visit here— were rejected. That was our fault for not doing a better job identifying legitimate academic prospects, but it still hurt.

Now, we process a much higher percentage of admissible recruits because we do a better job of identification—not because any standards have been reduced. Those standards still are the same as they were five years ago, or 10 years ago. The same people still read and judge the applications. In fact, we have higher SAT averages on the team now than we did when we arrived in 1992.

I've come to believe there's one more part to the jigsaw—breathing life into it.

One of my favorite expressions is, "Man will do so much for a dollar, and more for another man—but he'll die for a cause." This is a driving statement for me. A cause is the glue that binds the puzzle together, the blood that surges through it to bring it to life.

Creating a cause, something to zealously invest in, is the most fundamentally important thing I can do. When I recruit, or when I speak with the players during the week or before games, I try to grab and capture the essence of the situation—with none of the frills.

My most fervent goal, my constant goal, is to create a cause that demands relentless dedication.

3.

High Hopes

*"Every time a football player goes out
to ply his trade, he's got to play from the ground
up—from the soles of his feet right up to his
head. Every inch of him has to play. Some guys play
with their heads. That's okay. You've got to be smart to be
number one in any business. But more important,
you've got to play with your heart—with every fiber of
your body. If you're lucky enough to find a guy
with a lot of head and a lot of heart, he's never
going to come off the field second."
—Vince Lombardi*

By the fall of 1995, our fourth season at Northwestern, I knew our persistence and mistakes and corrections had enabled us to weld together the borders of the puzzle. It had been painful, but we had put together much of the image we had imagined. What I didn't know was that the vision was ready to hop off the box top and come to life.

Beginning in my second season, 1993, I enlisted Steve Musseau, who was 71 at the time, to come to Camp Kenosha every year. He has the peaceful, inspiring presence of Gandhi, and he immediately became a significant part of our program.

What Steve does is teach how the mind works. How we think, how we learn, how we store things. His greatest lesson is that vividly imagined events and activities actually can be more productive than physically practiced ones, because anything vividly imagined becomes the truth to your mind.

I had gotten to know Steve when I was coaching at Air Academy High School in Colorado, where two of his sons played for me, and he had become like a mentor to me. Steve had been a very successful head coach at the University of Idaho, and then he started his own motivational positive self-image company.

Steve had credibility as a motivational source: He's had cancer, four quadruple heart bypasses, and diabetes, among other medical conditions. I wasn't sure if he'd even live through the week I was asking him to come to Kenosha; I now think we've helped keep him alive.

In Colorado I had gotten caught up in what he did, so I had him put our high school teams through his 16-hour seminar. For a high school team to go through that, well, that's pretty different. But he had so many good things to say, and I loved the way he delivered it all.

He taught me how to vividly paint a picture with words and how important positive reinforcement was—not just the things others say to you, but the things that you say to yourself. It was from him that I learned the Ahab story, which I'll tell later, and visualization techniques.

I consider the intimate details of our visualizing to be pretty private, but I will say I lead the Northwestern team through a voluntary session after every Thursday night meeting. It seems like an amazing amount of our better players stay for it.

We begin by turning out the lights in the room and having a relaxation period, and then I try to evoke all the senses. You want to hear, feel, see, smell and taste what the next game will be like. I'll talk through the entire scenario, from arriving at the stadium and getting dressed ... to seeing the crowd start filing in ... to walking off victorious. I ask them to visualize the most difficult task they'll have to take on in the game—and picture themselves getting their body in position to make that play.

We wanted to build confidence, build purpose and build a system, and Steve's skills would be paramount in that effort. The first year Steve came, his emphasis was on trust. The second year, his thrust was patience. The third year, his lesson was faith, and he began that delivery a little differently.

Prior to our first 1995 season meeting in August, we posted flyers around the Nicolet Center that said, "Belief Without Evidence." There was no explanation along with the signs. It was just statement after statement, flyer after flyer. We put them in the coaches' rooms, in the hallways, in the weight rooms, wherever any of us would go.

As I stood before our players at the preseason meeting, a man tapping a cane and wearing a long wig, long robe and sandals walked into the auditorium. He started down the aisle, and I just looked at him with my mouth open.

The players saw me respond and turned to look at him as well. They burst out with laughter. It took them a few seconds to realize who it was, but the guys who had been there for two or three years knew. So I said, "Coach Musseau?" And he answered, "No. Moses!"

"Moses?"

"That's right."

"What are you doing?"

He said, "I've been lost in this desert since 1971, and I'm damned tired of it and I'm here to lead us out." Then he walked up on stage where I was. He put in a tape of Frank Sinatra singing "High Hopes," and of course, there were smirks and snickers. Most of our guys didn't even know who Frank Sinatra was, and the freshmen particularly were bewildered by this scene.

With that song playing in the background, Steve went into an oration about "Belief Without Evidence," and he defined it as meaning "faith." He recalled that in '93 we'd talked about trust, and that in '94 we'd talked about patience. Now, he said, we're in the final step: faith. Then he said, "I want you all to stand up, and I want you all to sing this song."

He rewound "High Hopes" and played it again, and a few guys muttered along. That wouldn't do. Steve scolded us and said, "Not good enough," and played it again.

Steve has some trouble hearing, so he must have repeated it five times before the entire group, players, coaches, everyone, was singing to his satisfaction. In fact, we were singing our lungs out. He then announced we were going to sing this every night.

So every night of the preseason, we'd end practice by singing "High Hopes." By the time we got through the 19 days, we had all kinds of offshoots of it. Some guys had dances for it, some guys would wave their hands, and some had their own little rap mix to it.

The song gave us a theme and a value. We now were playing on trust, patience and faith. That's what we had to do. Because, honestly, there was no tangible reason for us to believe we could beat Notre Dame in the first game or have the kind of year we were going to have. There was no evidence.

Steve also had each of us write down affirmations, including a group affirmation and two of our own. The one he had us all write was, "I easily find ways to put myself and others up." One I chose for myself was, "I am and will be in total control." That was what I saw as my role, and I knew I had to consciously work on that. Control didn't always come naturally for me.

At that meeting, I got emotional in saying it was time for us to have a big-time defense. I meant that, I knew that, and I think our kids took that to heart. Then I took out a set of balancing scales.

I designated one side of the scale to represent Northwestern and the other to be Notre Dame. I told the team that there were 19 practice days available to each team, so I put 19 pennies on the Northwestern side and 19 on the Notre Dame side.

(Pennies don't all weigh the same, it turns out, so I had to play around a bit to get just the right combination of pennies. Otherwise, they wouldn't weigh out evenly. That took a lot more work than I thought it would, and I ended up having to adjust the scale a bit to balance it. But I got it there.)

"There's nothing we can do about Notre Dame in the next 19 days," I said. "The only thing we can control is our own practices and how hard we go at it." I took one penny off the Northwestern side, and, naturally, the scales tilted in favor of Notre Dame. "If you take one day off," I said, "that's what's going to happen, assuming Notre Dame makes the most of its 19 days."

We left 19 pennies on the Notre Dame side and emptied our side. After that, if we practiced properly, I'd end our meeting every night by putting a penny on our side of that scale—and then we'd sing "High Hopes." The players would just go nuts.

At one point, we'd scheduled a morning off up at Kenosha, and practice the day before reflected it. Their anticipation left the players distracted, and I didn't think they practiced hard enough to earn the penny. So I didn't give it to them. They were really taken aback, and some of the seniors said, "Coach, can we practice tomorrow?" I hesitated, but then I told them I'd allow it.

They practiced the next day the way I always want them to: like their hair's on fire. And when we got into the meeting that night, the first thing they wanted to know was if they'd earned their penny. They had practiced exceptionally well, so I put two pennies on the scale.

Practice actually went exceptionally well the entire preseason, and as a result we had some significant developments: With Steve Schnur taking over as the clear No. 1 quarterback, our offense began to have a chemistry I'd never seen before and was really starting to gel.

Defensively, our speed had become excellent and we were more physical than we had ever been. It helped that our secondary featured four guys who were in their third seasons as starters.

The weather got to be a mess in Kenosha, but it didn't impede us. In years past, I'm sure it would have. But our attitude was superior now, and that made things that once would have been crippling seem like minor inconveniences. When we got back to campus we had our final scrimmage and elected our captains: safety William Bennett, punter—and former walk-on—Sam Valenzisi, and linebacker Pat Fitzgerald.

By now, we were pretty heavily into the Notre Dame game plan. Actually, I had been pretty heavily into it for a long time. For my 49th birthday that spring, Mary got me two books on handling aging and another on Lou Holtz, the Notre Dame coach.

From what I read in Lou's book, I sensed he was really going to drive his team this season, and maybe too hard. They were coming off a bad year, by their standards, with a 6-4-1 record, including a 41–24 loss to Colorado in the Fiesta Bowl.

I had a feel for what Lou was doing in the spring, because we subscribe to the newspapers around South Bend and the *Chicago Tribune* writes a lot about them. So I had a feel for what he was doing in the preseason, too. He had taken the team to Culver Military Academy, about an hour south of the Notre Dame campus. It was miserably hot that summer—many people died in Chicago—and the team was staying in a place that was not air-conditioned.

We hadn't needed air conditioning the first three years at Kenosha, because it's so much cooler up there, but we needed it in 1995. And we had it. To be in such uncomfortable conditions at Culver could have seemed like punishment to the Notre Dame players, and I sensed that was a mistake that might hurt their morale. I thought it might create an atmosphere that you wouldn't want as a coach.

In my opinion, you can push and push players on the field as long as they can count on basic human comforts like eating and sleeping well. But it's hard to build your team's spirit when the players are uncomfortable in their rest time, and they can start to question your decisions. I have no idea if it came to pass that way at Notre Dame, but I felt there was a chance they would not be unified when we played.

I've always liked Lou, but I'm not so sure he thought very highly of me—if he even thought of me at all. It's not like I'd done a lot to earn his respect, but when you open the season up against the same team four straight years, you'd think he would at least know who the other team's coach is.

That spring I was waiting for a flight at O'Hare Field when I noticed Coach Holtz sitting about, oh, three chairs away from me. I thought perhaps he hadn't seen me. So I got up and said, "Lou, how you doing?"

He said, "Hey, Jerry. Where are you now?" I didn't know quite what to say, but I didn't want to embarrass him. So I mentioned that I was waiting for Vince Okruch, who used to work for Lou, and I figured he'd know that Vince was at Northwestern now.

I'd hardly gotten the words out of my mouth when up walks Vince, and I'm sure Lou then put together that I was the Northwestern coach. He wasn't sure who I was, but he knew I was at Northwestern.

That was just the first episode, though. A few weeks later, a friend sent me a newspaper interview with Lou that I hadn't seen. One of the questions he was asked was, "Is it hard work preparing for Northwestern in an opening game?"

His remarks were to the effect of, "Well, it's hard blocking ghosts. You don't know what Northwestern is going to do on offense. They may be in a two-back set, they may go in a one-back set, or they may even use the no-backs set like they did when Gary Barnett used to be there."

A few days later, SportsChannel taped Lou's TV show from a bar on the south side of Chicago. They asked him about their game with us, and he said, "I want you to know, I have a great deal of respect for Leon Burtnett."

Which was fine, except Leon Burtnett was the name of a former Purdue coach. They had to stop him and say, "Coach, his name is Gary Barnett." They taped over that, so it never got on the air, but somebody there called to tell me about it.

On Monday before the game, I gave out the scouting report. The cover page said, "Belief Without Evidence." I told the team, "We're healthy. We're rested. We're prepared. We're focused, anxious and hungry." And we were.

Practice that week was clean, crisp and businesslike. These

players had a sense about themselves, and it didn't matter a bit that oddsmakers had made Notre Dame almost 30-point favorites.

Notre Dame, as Lou pointed out, was thinking more about its entire season than its opening game. In an interview I remember him saying, "We don't have the luxury" of just concentrating on Northwestern. I played that part of the interview for the team—and rewound it and replayed it a time or two.

We knew the College Football Hall of Fame had just opened in South Bend, so we made arrangements to tour there the Friday afternoon before the game. It turned out to be better than I'd imagined it could be. It was an incredible adventure. If you haven't been there, you've got to go.

The kids got a real sense of the rich history of the game of college football and how big the game is. It was so touching that Steve Musseau cried as he went through. There was a computer on display that included the all-time lettermen on every team, and the guys checked, "Missouri, '68" for my name.

One exhibit was a replica of a locker room with coaches giving speeches. There was also an interactive training center. On display were jerseys from our Colorado team the year we won the national championship, as well as the school banners of the *Associated Press* Top 25.

The tour gave me a deep, uplifted feeling, almost a tingle. When we were leaving, Bernie Kish, the director, said, "You know, I think you guys are going to beat Notre Dame." When we moved into and up the rankings later, Bernie sent us a picture every week of where our school flag was in their Top 25 display.

We were pretty jacked up when we left the Hall of Fame, and we went right to Notre Dame Stadium for a light workout. The place has an aura that I wanted to dispel immediately. So the first thing I did when we arrived was to assemble the kids and walk off 100 yards, to show them the field was regulation length. Then we walked off 53 yards, to show them it was regulation width.

"What do you know—same as ours," I said. Then I said, "Now, look in the grass. Do you see any ghosts here?"

That must have made for quite a sight, 120 people looking through the grass for ghosts. Nobody saw any, though, so we began practice. When we walked through the runway afterward, Jeff Genyk, our coordinator of football operations, pointed out a penny. I picked it up.

That night, we had the phones in our Michigan City hotel removed from the players' rooms. Most hotels have the capacity to just shut down the long-distance call-making possibilities, but this one didn't. So we asked our captains if they wanted to leave the responsibility with each player or to have the phones physically removed. They wanted the phones out.

This might not sound like much of anything, but to me it was a sign of focus. The first thing young athletes do when they get in their rooms is get on the phone. We got a phone report from our '94 trip to Iowa, and we had guys getting calls at two and three in the morning. That kind of stuff is not conducive to winning football, and we ended up having the phones taken out in every hotel last season.

We met as a team before we left for the stadium in the morning—that's when I try to get the last really thoughtful messages across so they have time to absorb them. I got out the scales and put the 19 pennies on each side. It was balanced. "We assume Notre Dame did everything it could," I said, "and we've earned our 19."

Then I took out the penny Jeff had found, and I said, "But we practiced the Sunday before we left for Kenosha, and that was actually one more time than they did." I put that penny on our side, and the scaled tilted to us.

Then I said, "I do not want you to carry me off the field after this game. I want you to act like you've been here before, like you've done this before and you're used to this."

It was a powerful moment. We then had about a 35-minute ride from Michigan City to the stadium, and I told them I didn't want them to play the game before we got there and get their necks all tensed up. I wanted them loose and relaxed.

When we took the field, we were absolutely ready. Right away our defense was dominant, and our offense went according to script. We went ahead 7–0 on Schnur's perfect six-yard pass to wide receiver David Beazley, who punctuated the touchdown by crashing into the Notre Dame band.

The game went back and forth a little, but I never felt like we weren't in control. We led 10–9 at halftime because they missed an extra point, and then Schnur hit another one of our receivers, D'Wayne Bates, for a touchdown early in the third quarter. Notre Dame scored with 6:16 left but failed on a two-point conversion attempt when their center stepped on the quarterback's foot coming out of the snap.

At least officially that's what happened.

After the game a lot of our kids thought Ron Powlus had been tripped by someone else: Marcel Price, our defensive back who had been killed in a shooting over the summer. We wore his nickname, "Big Six," on patches on our jerseys all season. We took his jersey with us to every game and hung it up before the kids walked out of the locker room.

In every meeting we had before a game, I'd ask the kids to play one play for Marcel—who was a delightful kid. I didn't care when they did it, but if they were in there I wanted them to pick one play ahead of time and play it for Marcel and bring him with us.

Notre Dame still had plenty of time to score again, though, so we needed to run out the clock. We gave the ball up quickly after we got it back but held them on a fourth and 2 when Matt Rice, one of our defensive tackles, stuffed their running back Randy Kinder.

When we got the ball back this time, we had a third and about 7 to deal with. We couldn't decide what to run, so I said, "Steve, what do you want to throw?" He said, "660 X Firm," which was basically a curl route. That wasn't necessarily what I thought was the play to go with, but what mattered was it was the one that Steve was most confident in executing.

Sure enough, he fired it in to D'Wayne, who made a great catch. Then running back Darnell Autry ran about 30 yards, only to be ridiculously called for taunting. But the first down was what mattered. The clock ran out, and we had won 17–15.

No one tried to carry me off the field, and—out on the field—the guys acted like we had won just another game. It wasn't like it was the end-all, although I later found out that Valenzisi had scooped out some of the Notre Dame grass as a souvenir.

Once we got in the locker room, though, we became idiots. Absolute fools. Everybody went crazy. We were dancing, screaming, laughing. It was a hoot. We were giddy. I think one of our tight ends, Shane Graham, tried to kiss everybody on the team.

I went out to the press tent to do interviews, and I made the point that this season was a marathon, not a sprint. Coach Holtz was very gracious after the game, and funny, too:

"The kicking game was pretty good, other than the missed [extra points]," he said. "Which is like, 'Other than the assassination, how was the play, Mrs. Lincoln?' "

On my way back to the locker room one of the radio guys from Chicago stopped me and asked if I could go on with them live right away. We needed those kinds of things, and I'd always had a good relationship with the guy who asked, so I said, "Okay." Well, it took forever for the host to come on the phone, and when he did his lead statement was like, "The perennial losers of Chicago ..."

That set me off. I just stopped and said, "What kind of bull is this?" I gave the phone back to the guy I knew and refused to do the interview. I wasn't going to listen to that kind of stuff before, and I wasn't going to listen to it now.

You know, if you don't say something to somebody in that situation they'll just go ahead and keep beating up on you. I guess it's a respect thing. At least that's the way I was taking it.

My son, Clay, had had a game the night before, so Mary had stayed behind in Evanston to watch him. But my daughter, Courtney, was at the game, and I was looking for her as soon as I came out of the locker room. It seemed like all 60,000 people at the game were right outside the locker room, though, and I couldn't find her right away. When I did, well, it was pretty neat to be able to hug her.

Greg Meyer, our offensive coordinator, had his family at the game. Afterwards, his little daughter Makenzie said, "Mom, why are all these people on the field?" Greg's wife, Daryl, explained that Northwestern had beaten Notre Dame. Makenzie said, "Wait till I tell my dad that they beat Notre Dame!" Greg said he needed to spend a little more time at home and let his daughter know what he does for a living.

I called Mary from my cellular phone on the bus on the way back, and it was one of the sweetest rides I've ever had. I just had this grin stuck on my face, and all these cars with Northwestern people in them buzzed around us, honking and waving their flags. It was a triumphant return. School wasn't even in session yet, but we probably had a thousand fans waiting for us back in Evanston.

Rodney Ray, a defensive back who'd come such a long way as a person, got off the bus and went over and sat on his car and watched all the hoopla unfold. I went over to Rodney and asked him what he thought. He shook his head and said, "Never thought I'd see the day."

We really hadn't eaten—those cold chicken meals we get after the game have got to stop—so I had all the coaches and their families over for pizza that night. Our answering machine flat out died in the next few hours, so I was on the phone almost all night.

When the pizza man arrived, the guy said, "Is this Coach Barnett's house?" and asked if he could meet me. We were all gathered in the living room watching highlights, and he came in and shook my hand. We all high-fived him. He stayed a while, as a matter of fact.

When I went to the coaches' convention in Dallas in January, I got on the shuttle to the Marriott. I was the only passenger on the shuttle when it picked me up, and at the next stop who should get on but ... Lou Holtz.

He gets on, puts his stuff down, turns around and never even looks at me. I thought, "I don't believe this. You've got to be kidding me."

Then he looks up, smiles and goes, "Hey, Gary, how you doing?" We had a good talk.

4.

Miami Vise

One significant test of quality leadership is how
well the leader copes with disappointments, defeat, or
some form of overriding adversity. Voltaire,
in praising this quality in the Duke of Marlborough,
called it, "Calm courage in the midst of tumult,
that serenity of soul in danger, which is the greatest
gift of nature for command."
—Anonymous

"Upset of the Century" was the headline in the *Chicago Sun-Times* the day after the Notre Dame game, and the paper later came out with T-shirts printed with the game score and the words, "Do You Believe in Miracles?"

They sent us about 150 of those, but I refused to wear the shirt or let our kids wear them because I didn't like our accomplishment being classified as a miracle. I'm sure the *Sun-Times* meant well, but that statement insulted what we had done, and accepting that mentality could undermine what we were trying to achieve.

Regardless, it became a carnival atmosphere around Evanston over the next few days. On Sunday afternoon, I went down and did a piece on the Fox Network's NFL pre-game show. Steve Schnur was on *Good Morning, America* on Monday. All of a sudden, everybody wanted to talk to us. The media requests more than quadrupled.

That was understandable. We really didn't deserve the attention before. I had noticed how little media coverage we usually got, but I didn't carry any resentment about it. We had two weeks until our next game against Miami of Ohio, so we gave the kids Monday and Tuesday off. That was good, because it gave us all time to cope with this rush of attention.

We knew we would have to be able to throw the ball against Miami of Ohio, because they played basically a nine-man front and heavily supported their run defense. It was going to be critical for us to be able to throw deep and force them out of that, and we knew that would pose some problems for us.

Miami plays in the Mid-American Conference, which might not have a glamorous name but is known for hard-nosed football. If you let down against a MAC team, you really make yourself vulnerable. We knew that, though, and we weren't overconfident—at least it didn't seem that way. I don't think there was anybody who got too caught up in the Notre Dame game.

I know people feel now that we must have been riding too high after Notre Dame, but it wasn't perceptible during our preparation. The players had handled all the questions with humility, and they didn't have any cockiness to them at all. I mean, what right did we have to be cocky, anyway?

One of our alums had given me a quote, and it went something like, "The victory was sweet, we drank our full, but we know there is still work to be done." We all felt that way. I put that on the cover of our scouting report, but I don't think I even had to.

The players, to me, were just as hungry for the Miami game as they had been for the Notre Dame game, and we were well-prepared on both sides of the ball. I wouldn't change a thing we did in those two weeks. I never sensed anything was going wrong.

I do think, however, we had a problem with our confidence level swelling during the Miami game itself.

Before the game, I addressed meeting our team goals and stressed that we still were in phase one: obtaining the right attitude and chemistry. Part of achieving that, I told them, was to be able to handle this game.

As it turned out, part of achieving that was not being able to handle this game.

The game, our first at home in 1995, in front of a small crowd of 26,352, began with a moment of silence for Marcel Price.

Paul Janus, our special teams snapper, really hurt his shoulder early on and wasn't able to continue playing. So our second-string snapper, Larry Curry, who also starts at defensive tackle, was going to have to handle the snaps for punts, field goals and extra points. Larry had a lot of experience, so the change wasn't an immediate concern.

We went ahead 21–0 on three Schnur touchdown passes, two to D'Wayne Bates and one to Darnell Autry. Just before halftime,

40

though, Miami scored when Dee Osborne—a kid we recruited but didn't end up offering a scholarship—blocked a punt and recovered it in the end zone. We really had a blocking breakdown on our left side, and Larry's snap wasn't good but it wasn't terrible.

On Miami's first series of the second half, I was on the headset with our defensive coaches, and they felt like they knew Miami was going to run a three-step dropback pass on the next play because of what we knew about its offensive tendencies. We bluffed them with our defensive set, and Rodney Ray intercepted the pass and ran it back 20 yards for a touchdown. That made it 28–7.

The instant Rodney reached the end zone, though, I suspected we were in trouble.

On our sideline, guys were laughing and high-fiving and carrying on, and there were still 29 minutes left in the game. I could sense something coming. It was like being in a storm drain and not being able to find the plug. I didn't know how to stem it, because it was coming from everywhere and everyone.

We had a field goal attempt blocked after a bad snap. Then another bad snap kept us from even getting off another field goal attempt and Miami drove for a touchdown to make it 28–14.

Suddenly, our offense was stagnant, and our defense couldn't contain their backup quarterback, whose scrambling style we hadn't adequately prepared for. We were being outhustled and outhit—out-everythinged.

Miami drove for another touchdown with eight minutes left, and now it was 28–21. Then came an 80-yard drive, and it was 28–27 with two minutes left. Miami went for two and didn't make it, so all we had to do was make a couple of first downs and we would still win because Miami was out of timeouts.

Well, we got one first down, but then it was fourth and 3 at our own 37 with less than a minute left. We had to punt.

For all the trouble Larry had been having, he had had a good punt snap in between. But Larry also had hurt his hand along the way, and he now was facing a psychological battle because of the bad snaps. We had a third snapper, but he had never done it in a game and I just wasn't confident in breaking him in this way. We had a great debate, but we decided to stay with Larry.

His snap hit the ground in front of Paul Burton and just took off. Instead of taking his hands all the way to the ground to stop it, Paul tried to short-hop it and it skimmed right between his legs. I don't think it ever got above turf level and it shot down to about the one-inch line before Paul jumped on it.

Now it was Miami's ball, right there, with 43 seconds left.

They tried a quarterback sneak on first down, but we stopped them. On second down, they tried the same thing but fumbled. They recovered, but they had to stop the clock by spiking the ball. And now it was fourth down with just a couple of seconds left. They came out to try the field goal and made it—despite a low snap—with no time left.

That was that: Miami of Ohio 30, Northwestern 28.

I really don't have the words to describe how I felt after that. I was angry, frustrated, completely disheveled. I didn't know what to think. I couldn't think straight. I saw Ron Vanderlinden, our defensive coordinator, roll his eyes into the back of his head. Defensive back Chris Martin threw his helmet down on the ground and it bounced up into the stands.

Maybe the only thing I did know at that moment was I wasn't going to stand for that. If we were going to lose, we were going to lose graciously and humbly. We were not going to act like it was somebody else's fault, or carry on about it. I went over to Chris and said, "That helmet had nothing to do with the loss, and it's not fair to treat it that way. And it's not fair to show your emotions that way. We're going to be gentlemen in victory and defeat."

We lost because Miami played the entire 60 minutes, and we played 30 or 35. We were not going to point fingers at anybody but ourselves, as a team. We were going to take this upon ourselves.

I felt terrible for Larry Curry, because we had put him in a bad position and he just had a bad day. The last thing I did in the locker room was approach Larry. Of course he was just devastated. I said, "Larry, you can't give up on me now. We've been together four years." He said, "I'm not giving up on you, and you can't give up on us."

A reporter asked Rob Johnson, our center, what he would say to Larry, and in Rob's own way he refused to let anyone single out any of our players.

"That's a ridiculous question," he said. "If anyone else wants to ask any other questions about any particular person about this loss, we're done [with the interview]. There's 95 guys on this team, and every single one of them played a part in this loss. It's not Larry Curry, it's not Paul Burton."

It didn't seem possible that this could happen. After all we'd been through for four years to get to where we were, this was shattering. It was so alien, so unexpected, so humiliating, to lose that way. I guess the best word to describe my feeling was "traumatized."

We had our usual reception for our coaches and family and friends in our offices that night. That's a very difficult situation, because these games aren't life and death to your friends and family. They figure, "Shoot, we'll play another one next week."

But for a coach after a loss, well, a piece of you has died that won't grow back. It doesn't regenerate itself. You're often embarrassed and humiliated, and I was never more so than I was that night. When I walked up into our outer office, I immediately turned right down the corridor to my own office. I didn't want to see anybody or say anything to anybody.

Mary saw me come in and came into my office a moment later, and we sat down on the couch together. I don't remember my exact words to her, but I honestly didn't think I could ever coach again. I wish I could have cried, but I couldn't even muster the tears. I was so overcome.

It was like I didn't even know who I was.

Part Two:

Priming the Pump

5.

Growing Pains

"Until one is committed, there is hesitating, the chance to draw back, always ineffectiveness. Concerning all acts of initiative (and creation), there is one elementary truth, the ignorance of which kills countless ideas and splendid plans: that the moment one definitely commits oneself, the Providence moves, too.... A whole stream of events issues from the decision, raising in one's favor all manner of unforeseen incidents and material assistance which no man could have dreamed would come his way."
—*Johann Wolfgang von Goethe*

I was born in Lakeland, Florida, my mom's hometown and near where my dad, Leland, had been stationed in the Air Force. Dad got out of the Air Force when I was about a year old, and we went back to his hometown of Mexico, Missouri.

According to the signpost outside town when I was growing up, Mexico had a population of about 12,000 and was "The Firebrick and Saddle Horse Capital of the World." Now it just says, "Welcome to Mexico."

The major crop in the area was soybeans, which every year they'd honor with a soybean parade. One of our big thrills as kids was to get a peashooter and all the soybeans you could carry and try to hit the queens and other people riding on the floats.

Our kicks sometimes were hard to get: One summer, a grain elevator was being built in town. It had to be seamless, so the concrete poured continuously. We'd go get ice cream cones and just watch it pour. That ended up being good entertainment for about three months.

When I was about five, my uncle bought me a bright red, shiny football helmet. I loved that helmet. I wore it everywhere. Wore it

47

to bed, even. I absolutely loved the game of football, and I was the first one on my block with his own helmet.

My brother, Mike, who's two years younger than I, got an old leather helmet that was furry and worn. We'd play each other in the backyard, and I'd trick him into letting me wear the leather one when it was cold.

Life and *Look* magazines would run articles and beautiful pictures of college football, and I kept scrapbooks of all the Notre Dame guys and Army and Navy teams. Air Force had just started a team, and I remember one Christmas my dad getting me a white helmet with a snap-on facemask like theirs.

That helmet was something else. It made you look like a fighter pilot, and I took it and painted on lightning bolts and No. 35—for my favorite player, the great running back Hank Kuhlmann at Missouri. As Boy Scouts, we'd go over and serve as ushers at Mizzou games in Columbia at least once a year. I was there every chance I got.

My dad went to work for Libby's canned goods as a traveling salesman, and as often as I could I'd ride shotgun with him over all the dusty roads on the way to Moberly, Hannibal or Kirksville. It was a joy to get to eat in restaurants with him. To go out for a hamburger and some pie, well, in those days that was a big deal. We had an A&W Root Beer stand in Mexico that we could go to every Friday. When I visited my mom there this summer, we ended up at a Golden Corral, but to this day I have a fondness for A&W—and we would have gone to the A&W if it had still been there.

We didn't really have Little League in Mexico, but we had a town recreation baseball league during the summer. You'd bring your lunch and play a couple of times a day. Once a year, everybody in the league got to make the two-hour trip to St. Louis for a Cardinals' game at old Sportsman's Park. I'd get a new pair of jeans for the occasion—always a big day in my life. When the Cardinals batted in the ninth inning, you'd take your seat and flap it up and down to make noise. We'd eat hot dogs until we got sick. One time the great Red Schoendienst did a little clinic for us, and he gave me his glove. That was amazing.

We didn't have uniforms, so for the night we'd play under the lights at Green Field in Mexico, I'd get a new pair of jeans and a sleeveless white T-shirt. My mother always said it was because there would be a lot of people watching those games. You'd get your cap for the summer, whatever color you wanted—but with no logos or labels—at Fredendall and Wilkens department store.

On days we didn't play baseball we played golf—on sand

48

greens. I never played on grass greens until we moved to St. Louis a few years later, and then it was too expensive to play often.

Sports were the good part of my life. But, in truth, they were an escape because I was terribly uncomfortable for a long time. It was almost traumatic in some ways. I was chunky and wore glasses, but my real distress came from being a bedwetter.

That didn't really end until my sophomore year at Parkway High in St. Louis, and it was hell. I'd get up and try to hide the sheets, but you just couldn't hide them. My dad would threaten to hang them out the window—he may even have gone ahead and done it; somehow, I can't remember—or put the mattress in the front yard.

I ended up having the plastic sheets and all. Of course, I couldn't go spend the night at friends' houses. I was pretty consistent with it, and I never did find out why it happened. I survived it, but I was pretty fragile for a long time.

But moving to St. Louis after ninth grade really changed my life. This might sound funny, but there was almost a caste system in place in Mexico. I knew I wouldn't get out of there. My parents didn't make a lot of money, and I never quite felt accepted there.

At Parkway High in St. Louis I met a girl named Mary Weil, and she describes me as a nerd then. She says I told a lot of dumb jokes and giggled a lot. We met in the band, where I was playing saxophone. I hated the sax. I only played it because my dad was a good saxophone player. He could pick it up and blow.

During the summer between my sophomore year and my junior year at Parkway, I grew about four inches, got contact lenses and my whole world changed. Mercifully, the bedwetting had stopped the night before my first high school ballgame.

All of a sudden, girls who would never look at me before were hanging on my arm. A few of us from nerdsville got close to one another, and then we got cool. I became the varsity quarterback—even if it did mean I had to pitch the ball to Terry Plunkett so he could throw it.

That winter, Mary and I went on our first date—January 12, 1963. Bowling. And I knew right away she was it. I mean, I knew. I was smitten. I'd been wanting to ask her out ever since the day we had to share a chair in a class.

We went undefeated my senior year in football, and our coach was Jack Wells. I didn't know what an influence he would be until I later was trying to decide what to do with my life. When it came to it, I said, "Who's the happiest guy that I know?" And the answer was Jack Wells. He always made the game fun. He always listened. Whatever you said meant something to him.

I only remember seeing him mad once or twice, and I kind of brought one of those on myself by foolishly trying to fake a punt on fourth and something like 22 late in a game against Clayton. I want to say I was kind of goofy and out of it from being hit earlier in the game, but either way we gave the ball to Clayton deep in our territory and nearly lost because of it. Luckily, our defense held and our undefeated season wasn't ruined.

When the game ended, I looked over at the sideline and saw my dad and Jack Wells, side-by-side, coming right at me. I kept my helmet on, because I knew it was not going to be good. I'm glad I kept it on. They blistered me. A couple of other dads I knew let me hear about it pretty good, too.

Back then, college recruiting was much different than it is now. Coaches would just come by after the season was over. You never got phone calls, and there wasn't this rushed, crazy competition for spots.

During my senior year, after a game against Brentwood, some guy grabbed me and said he was a scout for Missouri and wanted me to know I had played a great game. Until then, I had not even thought about college, and I doubt I would have gone without somebody approaching me about it.

I was in class one day after the season when Coach Wells pulled me out and said a coach from Kansas State was there to talk to me. His name was John Kadlec, and he said, "Gary, I want to offer you a scholarship." I was a pretty shrewd negotiator. I said, "You're kidding me! A full scholarship?"

So I took a trip up to Kansas State, and, jeez, I was excited. I also visited Kansas, unofficially, and really loved that campus. But then Hank Kuhlmann came to recruit me for Missouri. *The* Hank Kuhlmann, my childhood hero. I couldn't believe it.

I went down to Columbia, and, as it turned out, had a miserable time. I went to a fraternity party where I didn't know anybody, and I felt like a little kid. But it didn't make any difference. I had been watching Missouri football all my life, and that was where I was going to go. Later, Alabama, Illinois, Baylor, and Vanderbilt came by to see me, but I told Coach Wells I didn't want to talk to anybody else.

The night before the signing party in downtown St. Louis I broke my ankle playing basketball. I showed up in a cast at the signing, and the Missouri coach, Dan Devine, was upset. I don't know if it had anything to do with the circumstances of our first meeting, but I never felt I managed to gain his respect as a football player.

In those days, freshmen weren't eligible for varsity. We only had two games as freshmen, and the rest of the time we just sort of beat each other up. Knowing that was coming, I didn't show up on campus in the kind of condition I should have been in. I had a good spring practice as a defensive back, but they red-shirted me the next fall and plugged me in at linebacker.

All I did was wear these monkey suits with padding on my arms and legs—I looked like the Michelin Man—and line up for All-American offensive tackle Francis Peay to work over. He would just hound you, but he did it with class. Some of the other guys would try to hurt you, but Francis would just do what he had to do. I'm not sure you could get away with making a player a human dummy today, but it was common then.

I put on some weight and had a really good sophomore spring at linebacker, but I got hurt and missed the spring game. They wanted me to put on even more weight for the fall, but I didn't want to. I already felt fat as it was.

Instead, I went from 216 pounds to 187—and got moved to receiver. The coaches weren't happy with me, and I just kind of flopped around that season. By spring, though, I was pretty good. I had something like 11 catches in one scrimmage, and I thought I would have a chance to crack the lineup the next fall.

But on my way home that night I heard Coach Devine on the radio. Somebody called and said, "Hey, how about this kid Barnett?" And he said, "Well, he's a pretty good spring player, but he's just never any good in the fall." That bothered me, but I kept at it and by the end of spring I was alternating on the first team.

Then my 21st birthday rolled around and I went out to celebrate and got my fanny in trouble. It wasn't anything so terrible, but it was bad enough that I don't want to say any more about it. Mostly, it was stupid, absolutely stupid.

So Devine had to rescue me, only he didn't really rescue me and now I was on his bad list. I was in the doghouse, big time. Initially, my scholarship was taken away. I ended up on the scout team, again, but I busted my butt against another All-American, our defensive back Roger Wehrli, every day.

College football might not have been all I had hoped for in personal glory, but I loved the game. Loved it all. Loved the guys, loved Missouri football. I would do it all over again, except the part where I got myself in trouble, because I always believed I was contributing and was part of the whole scene.

One of the assistant coaches, Clay Cooper, really took to me. For some reason he never had me do penalty runs and things like that. When one of our defensive backs got hurt my senior year, Coop called me in to ask who the toughest cover guy was for me as a receiver. I told him, and that's who played. I'm not saying that's why, but it meant a lot to me that he asked. My son is partly named after Coop.

My dad had a heart attack the night before the Oklahoma State game that season. I called Coop, and he told me to go St. Louis and that he'd cover for me. I saw my dad, and I returned Saturday in time for the game. I got to play that day, and I just know my father heard my name on the radio. We won the Gator Bowl that year, and the guys from that team sent me a letter this past fall. A really nice letter.

At Missouri, I also developed special friendships in my fraternity, Beta Theta Pi. That association really smoothed down a lot of my rough edges, because I got to be around people who were successful in areas outside of sports. I learned how to dress, and I learned how to really appreciate people's talents in different areas—such as academics. I hadn't been exposed much to that.

Mary and I got married during March of my junior year, shortly after I had become eligible for the draft because I had gotten behind in my school hours. I flunked the draft physical because of scoliosis. I was relieved to be disqualified at the time, but I later wanted to join the Marines and the back problems came back to haunt me.

The following year, I was taking an American military history course from Dr. Alan Millett, and he convinced me that the thing to do was join the Marines and become an officer. He had been a Marine and thought I had a Marine mentality, and I believed in him because he was such a great teacher. But when I tried to petition the Marine Corps, I still couldn't get past the physical.

Graduation brought with it a period of enormous confusion for me. I applied to law school and got admitted to Missouri, but I wasn't going to be able to go until the next January so I took a couple of jobs to support us in between.

That fall was my first without football—unless you count playing in a flag league in St. Louis—and it was killing me. Missouri went to the Orange Bowl that year, while I was wondering what to do with my life.

All I seemed to be able to do was eliminate options: Law school somehow didn't seem like the true answer, and I didn't have an aptitude for selling insurance or vacuum cleaners—both of which I briefly tried. In fact, the only vacuum cleaner I sold was the one I had to buy for demonstrations.

During this time I got to thinking about who I knew that was truly happy—and Jack Wells. The more I thought about it, the more I knew I wanted to be like him. His background was as a counselor, so I applied to Missouri's counseling and pupil services program in the School of Education. I got my master's in education, and the program profoundly changed my life.

That's when I learned who I was. That's when I learned listening skills, and how your behavior can affect others. That's when I learned the concept of "discovery learning," which is really the truest form of learning. The light goes on for somebody when you allow them to discover the answer rather than providing it for them.

It's also where I learned the significance of empathy. You can't just say, "I'm going to be empathetic." It has to become an entire way of operating. You come to understand that in order to really be sincere, you have to be empathetic. It isn't a decision to change or affect somebody else's behavior but just a way to show you are sincere about your interest in people.

Other than my marriage, I don't think anything has changed my life more than those courses. I was learning about how you can affect people's lives and how you can help them. It was a fascinating new world, and I embraced it.

I was captivated by the curriculum and motivated academically for the first time. There was no way I was getting less than an A in a class. Part of my motivation probably came from the fact that it was the first time I had ever paid for my own courses, which makes me think of the downside of scholarships: You tend to take everything for granted. You don't fully appreciate things unless you're paying for them yourself.

One of my classes required me to go to a grade school and work with a kid who had lost a parent. I got to know a boy who lived in a wretched area. We'd go to the Missouri Lakes and walk around, or frog hunt, or just sit a little bit. I really helped him, I know I did. I don't know if I've ever had a better feeling than that.

Coach Devine had allowed me to be a graduate assistant coach in the spring of 1971. I didn't get any money, but I got the grey coaching gear. As much as I had missed football, it seemed odd to be dressing with the coaches.

I began wondering whether I should try to focus on becoming a famous shrink. The exciting thing to do would have been to go on and get a doctorate in clinical psychology.

Over spring break my friend Rick Unks wanted to go visit a cousin in Colorado. I had only been there once, a spontaneous and brief trip with some fraternity brothers, and Mary thought I should go.

The night before we left, though, I got food poisoning. I had never been so sick in my life, and I didn't think I could make the trip. However, I didn't want to let Rick down, so I went ahead.

Before we got out there, Rick had lined up about six coaching and counseling interviews for himself at different schools. I went along to talk to people, but I didn't bring any resumes or anything. For weeks, neither of us heard anything back, but I did get accepted to Missouri's clinical psych program and planned to enroll.

Then on May 11 I got a call from Air Academy High School, located on the Air Force base in Colorado Springs. They wanted to offer both of us assistant coaching jobs.

Somehow, it just seemed right.

Mary was at work when I went out to celebrate. I left a note on the door: "See you at the Village Inn—We're moving to Colorado!" When Mary got there, I played a John Denver song on the jukebox.

6.

Gathering Stones

"Old man," said a fellow pilgrim near,
"You are wasting your strength with building here,
Your journey will end with the ending day,
You never again must pass this way,
You have crossed the chasm deep and wide—
Why build you this bridge at the eventide?"

The builder lifted his old grey head,
"Good friend, in the path I have come," he said,
"There followeth after me today,
A youth whose feet must pass this way.
This swollen stream which was naught to me,
To that fair-haired youth may a pitfall be,
He, too, must cross in the twilight dim,
Good friend, I am building the bridge for him."
—Anonymous

Eastern Colorado looks a lot like Western Kansas—flat and bar-ren—and we only got that far after going through a little scare with our cat, Boston Blackie, who ran away for a few hours at a truck stop. Mary had been apprehensive as it was, and now she was really wondering what I had gotten us into.

But the minute we got to Colorado Springs, she loved it. It was a gorgeous setting. In the mountains, and mountains all around. We took an apartment that overlooked the Garden of the Gods and its two red stones that look like camels kissing.

For a salary of $8500, my job included teaching five classes of world history and helping coach baseball and football. It had been about a decade since Air Academy's football program had had a winning season.

At the time, my style was pretty much that of a yeller and a screamer. But it helped that I was aggressive. I put in the offense, and I was calling plays by the end of the season.

The first game I ever coached in, we tied Denver East. All the fans ran out on the field after the game, and all the girls were hugging the players. I just went berserk, screaming at people to get off the field. They were excited about a tie? I couldn't believe they were behaving that way. I was so angry at the players, so angry at the school. I can feel that moment to this day.

I was still planning on being a counselor, but you had to teach for two years before you could be certified as one in Colorado. I came to look forward to the counseling as much as football every day. What I enjoyed most about it was the chance to support and teach and help the kids to understand they were in control of their problems.

I'm not sure I was as dramatic or creative in the classroom as I was on the field, but I was really into the teaching, too. This was a pretty conservative area, a real cowboy area, and of course a lot of the students were military brats.

John Carlos and Tommie Smith had just stood on the victory stand and raised their fists in the black power salute at the 1968 Olympics in Mexico City, and I asked my students if anybody had taken offense to that. Almost the whole class stood up. Of course, I went haywire and took just the opposite, liberal approach. I needed to stir it up a little bit, but it was also my politics.

I taught the military history differently than perhaps the Air Force would have liked. I'd concentrate on the blunders or the human side rather than, say, the tactical and strategic aspects.

The kids, I think, were shocked by me. They didn't classify me as a hippie, but they thought I was pretty close.

My hair was a little long then. When I say long, actually, it probably wasn't any longer than it is now. But back then, that was long. Steve Musseau used to say it was the "Buster Brown" look.

When I was growing up, I always had to have a flat top. My dad made me get a crew cut every two weeks. At Missouri, I let it grow a little into this sort of surfer look. One of the coaches called me "Ringo." When I came home after my freshman year with that hair and my new skateboard, my dad called me some names that wouldn't be politically correct today and about threw me out of the house.

My dad was a hard-nosed guy. Had his own chair, very strict. We went round-and-round about a lot of things. I was the only guy who had a 12:30 curfew all through high school—which my son happened to have, too.

In the end, of course, my dad seemed to get smarter the older I got. Since I was the first in my family to go to college—I think going into the service and immediately having a family kept him from going—he was really proud of that. By the time I got into coaching, we had a tremendous relationship. He loved to come watch us play.

When Mary and I were driving back to Colorado after Christmas in 1980 we had a flat tire around 11 at night. This was Kansas in January, a chilly night. I got out to fix the flat, and all of a sudden there was this warm breeze. I said, "Mary, something seems like death."

When we got home, I walked in the door and the phone rang. It was my brother calling to say that dad had died around 11 that night. He was 57 years old.

At my dad's autopsy, they found he had small coronary arteries. He also was a smoker, with a Type A personality and a Midwestern diet, all of which reinforced a decision I'd made to mind my diet. By 1978, I basically had quit eating red meat.

Another thing I do to stay healthy is jog. When we moved to Colorado, a couple of guys on the team needed a push, so I thought it would be a good idea to help them get in shape by "running" with them. But I'm not a sprinter; I'm not even a real runner. A jogger is what I am.

I found that jogging really gave me a precious creative period of time. Now it's become almost the most important 30, 35 minutes of my day. I solve my problems then. I find solutions then. I always run before I talk to the team, because I feel most alert at that time.

You wouldn't know it to see me running, though. In Evanston, I do the same course every time, but I can't tell you one thing or one person I see the whole way. Probably if you asked me to go an extra 10 yards, it would kill me.

After two years as an assistant I got the head coaching job at Air Academy, one of the best high school coaching jobs in Colorado. I think there was another guy they really wanted, but they couldn't find a way to get him in as a teacher.

We didn't have any money in the budget so that summer I painted and mowed the field. Mary and I designed a helmet logo, and we applied them with contact paper. We also sewed the words, "We Want 'Em" on the back of our 60 jerseys. I had gotten that idea from a coach I'd seen speak at a clinic.

As gung-ho and young as I was, I was taking pretty much the Type-A, high-strung approach. I worked extremely hard at motivating, which I still do, but I'd like to think my ways are more refined now.

The week we were playing Coronado, we had an incident where 11 of our starters had been caught drinking. I suspended them for the game, so there was no way we were going to win. That didn't mean I wasn't going to try.

One of our coaches' nieces was a Coronado cheerleader, if I remember correctly, and I had an idea. I had one of our female students put on a Coronado cheerleading uniform, get cream puffs and put little flags bearing our players' numbers in each. Then I had her walk into our cafeteria and deliver the cream puffs to the players and say, "I want you to know this is what we think of your team."

You never know how much that kind of stuff works, but my theory is that you leave no stone unturned if it might present you with an advantage. Or help you create a cause. We beat Coronado on the last play of the game.

We'd play the Palmer Terrors every year, and their mascot was an Indian named Eagle Beak who was portrayed as having this huge nose. The first year, I dressed up like an Indian—headdress and everything—and rode into practice on a horse. The horse stopped and threw me off in the middle of all the players. We stopped using the horse.

But we had a player on our team named Pat Forde, who is now a columnist for the *Louisville Courier-Journal*. Pat's nose very much resembled Eagle Beak's. For the next three years during Palmer week the players would carry Pat around on their shoulders chanting, "Eagle Beak, Eagle Beak...."

To illustrate a point before another game, I took a ping-pong ball and pushed it into a large jar of pinto beans. As I pushed the ball down into the beans, I said, "There are going to be things out there that get you down. There are going to be plays where you don't feel like getting back up. But you know what ... ?"

Then I'd shake the jar, and the ball would rise a little—something to do with the density of the beans and the lightness of the ball; I had read it somewhere.

"... If you keep picking yourself up, about the fourth quarter ..."

I shook the jar more, and the ball shot up through the beans.

"... About the fourth quarter, you're going to pick yourself up and win the game."

At a magic store I found one of those pitchers that looks empty even when it's been filled with water. Our colors were blue and white, so I put blue water in it. Before a game I told the team, "There are going to be times when you don't think there's anything left to give. You're going to want to give up."

Then from the apparently empty pitcher I'd pour a little water out and say, "But if you reach down inside yourself and believe in yourself, there's always more." Then I poured more water out, drank it down and threw the glass against the shower room wall. It shattered—and there's just something about the sound of shattering glass that fires you up.

When I decided we were going to beat somebody, we were going to beat them. We were going to find a way. But motivation can get sticky, because you're usually dealing with a large audience and all individuals are motivated differently. You have to have a feel for who responds to what, and when you're in a group setting it's hard to always know the right dynamic.

I made at least one really wrong decision on a kid at Air Academy. I got on his case hard during a film session, to the point where his brother got very upset and his dad later was enraged. Normally I wouldn't take that tack unless I knew the kid could take it and that was what he needed. I made a mistake with that one. It's bugged me for a long, long time.

It usually takes quite a bit to tee me off, but whenever I get angry at a player or a situation it's not hard for me to explode at the time. I often really struggle with it afterwards, though, and wonder if I should have responded differently.

An example of a situation I feel I understood better was how I later handled Darian Hagan, our quarterback at Colorado. Hagan was immensely gifted and probably the only player I've ever coached who could go right to the field from the chalkboard and immediately execute something new. He was so bright, though, that he'd get bored in practice. So I had to create ways to get him to do the mundane technique work that needed to be done.

We had a five-minute session every day when the quarterbacks took snaps from center and just stepped different ways. Hags would get bored with it, so I took a basket and set it up about 40 yards from center and challenged him to take that snap and throw the ball in the basket.

I didn't care if he hit the basket or not. I was trying to make sure that he went through the snap work. It got to where he'd take extra snaps so he could take extra throws at the basket.

We won our league my first year as head coach at Air Academy, and we built a program that began to perpetuate itself. I was state coach of the year a couple of times.

After 1981, my ninth year as head coach, a decision to split the school district left me at a personal crossroads. I was uncomfortable about having to choose between schools, and each was going to be in a lower football division.

Besides, at the time I was debating about getting out of coaching to become a stockbroker. I wasn't making any money, and we had two children by now. Then a job opened at Fort Lewis College, in Durango.

Mary and I made the five- or six-hour drive down to Durango in my 280Z. It was a lot of fun to drive through the mountains, and everything went great in Durango, but on the way back we hit a snowstorm. I mean, a snowstorm. I'm talking more than a foot—and we're in this 280Z.

I got out to put the chains on the tires. I'd never put them on before, and I hooked them up in such a way that a piece of the chain would hit the car on every rotation. It was going, "bonk, bonk, bonk." We couldn't see anything, and we couldn't stop. This was around Wolf Creek, and people have died there in similar conditions.

Mary was crying, screaming, scared to death: "We're not going to make it this time. We're not going to make it." Somehow, we did.

Despite what could have been construed as an omen, Mary didn't flinch about me taking the job. In fact, she took the opposite stance: "Look, either you take this college job or you quit bellyaching about your job and how you want to coach spring football and all that stuff."

I needed a push, and she put me over the edge. So we took the job.

Fort Lewis had been a renegade program and hadn't had a winning season in years.

I arrived there just in time to meet with the team before the players left for the summer. I told them when they came back they'd be tested in the weight room and that backs would have to be able to run a mile under six minutes and linemen would have to be able to do it under 6:30. These kids were looking at me like, "Yeah, right, who are you?"

When they came back in the fall, not a single lineman made the mile time. My blood pressure went up, and I got a little red. By the time all the testing was over, only one guy on the team made his time.

In a fury, I blew my whistle, got the whole team in the stands, and read the players the riot act. I said, "You all know where your bags are. Now, we're going to run until I quit blowing the whistle. And if you quit before then, go get your bags and head home."

They ran 40 40-yard windsprints. Well, maybe "ran" isn't the right word. By the last one, every kid was crawling. Almost every kid threw up. They thought I was nuts. I was nuts. It might sound cruel, but it was just part of setting a standard. If you demand it, you'll get it. And nobody left that day. They all hung in there, and we won four games that year.

The next year almost everybody made their times.

Recruiting was interesting at Fort Lewis, which was a four-year NAIA school. I made some deals with a local hotel and an airline, so we recruited like the big boys did. We only had a $1200 recruiting budget so I went ahead and spent $3800 of my own money on recruiting. I'd drive all over and stay in hotels or stay with friends. In fact, I had to get rid of the 280Z and get a Subaru so I could get better gas mileage.

All of the expenditures led to me being audited that year. When I went to see the Internal Revenue Service guy, I had a box full of receipts. He said, "Now, you're a football coach—and you're claiming all these things?"

I had a receipt for everything. I wasn't even halfway through when he said, "Okay, forget it. Just get out of here."

My first recruiting class came in, and in 1983 we played a bunch of freshmen. We won only four games again, but it was apparent to me we had built a foundation. After I left that fall, in fact, Fort Lewis went on to win the next season's conference championship.

We had a good two years there, although we had a tragedy before the 1983 season.

I had given the kids a day off after a scrimmage to look for housing. I had a meeting scheduled for that afternoon, but a couple of kids called and said they needed more time to find apartments. So I postponed it.

In the movie *Butch Cassidy and the Sundance Kid*, the scene where Butch and Sundance jump off a cliff into the water was filmed in Durango. Well, during the time between the originally scheduled meeting and the one we ended up having, a few of the players went out to that site and did some jumps.

One of them went up the cliff a second time, tripped, and fell in—and nobody saw him. They couldn't find him. The police ended up dragging a net across the river and found him the next morning. I kept thinking, "If I hadn't moved that meeting ... "

That summer, I had worked at the University of Colorado's camp and was asked to make a motivational speech to the campers. I knocked them out. I was really good. That's how Bill McCartney came across me for the first time.

I can still tell you the speech almost word-for-word. It was on goal-setting. I said that if you're without a goal, you're like a missile without a target and you inevitably self-destruct. When you self-destruct, you destroy everything around you.

I talked about wanting things—like learning to drive a stick shift, and how confusing it is initially to have three pedals and only two feet. The first time you drive it, it's embarrassing. But you want so badly to learn to drive it that in a month you can drive with one arm around your girlfriend.

That desire is similar to when you're a little kid and you wake up in the middle of the night and have to go to the bathroom ... but you remember that a monster is under your bed. If you put your foot on the floor, it's going to grab you. So what are you going to do? You stand on the edge of your bed and you jump all the way to the doorway—or close to it. It's probably the farthest you will ever jump.

I also gave the example of going to your first horror movie. On the walk home, of course, any movement in the bushes sounded like someone about to pounce. By the time you got home, you had just run a 4.4-second 40-yard dash.

What is it that made you do all that? You simply created a fear, one that wasn't even there, but you made it real. You vividly imagined it, and it made your heart beat. By using your imagination, you can make unrealistic goals become realistic.

I started the speech off, though, with a story that I still begin many of my speaking engagements with:

There was an old Arab named Ahab, who had wandered lost in the desert for about four days. He had run out of food and water and had decided to give up. As he lay face down in the sand, expecting death at any moment, a voice booms out of the sky, calling his name.

The voice asks, "Ahab, how would you like to have all the clear, cool water you can drink, and all the fruits and nuts and berries that you can eat?"

Ahab replies, "I'd love that. But where would I find that here, voice?"

The voice says, "Ahab, you just have to trust me. Get back on your camel, and ride four miles due east. You'll come over a sand dune and you'll see all the cold, clear water you can drink and all the fruits and nuts and berries you can eat."

Ahab decides this is his only chance, to believe the voice. So he struggles to his camel and gets on it. Just as he's about to take off, the voice yells out, "Oh, Ahab, when you get there, you're going to see a lot of rocks, a lot of stones. I want you to fill your saddle bags with these rocks and stones."

Ahab doesn't understand why this is important, but in order to find this oasis he's willing to agree to anything. Then the voice adds, "Ahab, when you wake up tomorrow, you're going to be really, really happy, then you're going to be really, really sad."

This made no sense to Ahab, but he continued on his camel four miles due east. Sure enough, he comes over a dune and there's a beautiful oasis, with all the cool, clear water he could drink and all the fruits, nuts, and berries he could eat.

He jumps off his camel, drinks to his fill and eats as much as he can eat. Then he remembers that the voice had told him to pick up rocks. As he looks around, he sees acres and acres of grey stones. Good-for-nothing rocks. This makes no sense to Ahab, so he picks up two of the stones, puts them in his pocket, and falls asleep.

He wakes up the next morning in the desert sun, and as he stretches he remembers the voice said he was going to be really happy, then really sad. He doesn't feel either way. But then he looks out over the oasis and sees that the water and food are gone, and so are all the rocks. He reaches into his pocket to look at the two rocks he had collected, and as he pulls them out they turn into diamonds. He looks at them and says, "Wow! Wow! ... Oh, no!"

The minute I said, "Oh, no!" the kids knew what the moral of the story was.

I told them there are going to be a lot of things told to them and thrown out to them by their parents, teachers, and coaches that they won't immediately understand. They're going to look like grey stones. But you need to trust those people and believe if you pick up what they throw out, they can turn to diamonds.

This story always captures an audience, because it tells the audience that you're about to give them a diamond—even if they don't see it at first, they'll have reason to believe you're going to give it to them.

Anyway, the 500 or 600 kids there gave me a standing ovation. One of the Colorado assistants, Gerry DiNardo, taped the speech and gave it to Coach Mac.

After the season I was out recruiting in Boulder and I heard there was going to be an opening on Mac's staff. I stopped by his office and told him I'd like to speak to him about the job. He said, "You know what, you're a guy I'd be interested in." He said, "I'll call you Monday."

That was it. That was my job interview. He called me Monday and said, "You're the guy I want. I'm going to pray about it for a week and get back to you." He called me the next Monday and formally offered me a job as running backs coach.

As fast as I could, I got ready to leave for Boulder and stopped by the bank to use an ATM—and was out of money. So I had to borrow $50 from a friend, Mark Anderson. Susan Steele, a former neighbor of ours, picked me up at the Denver airport and drove me to Boulder.

Halfway to Boulder, I asked her to stop the car. I was so nervous I had to get out and throw up.

7.

A Metamorphosis

"I've never known a man worth his salt who in the long run, deep down in his heart, didn't appreciate the grind, the discipline. There is something in good men that really yearns for the discipline and the harsh reality of head-to-head combat. I don't say these things because I believe in the brute nature of man ... But I firmly believe that any man's finest hour—his greatest fulfillment to all he holds dear—is that moment when he has worked his heart out in a good cause and lies exhausted on the field of battle—victorious."
—Vince Lombardi

It was a major, major leap for me to go to big-time college football. It exceeded what I thought I could do. Colorado. The Big Eight.

A painful part of the leap, though, was learning to be an assistant, which I now see as essential in my development. Even in the two years I had been an assistant coach at Air Academy, I really was calling all the shots. I thought I knew everything.

So I'll never forget my first staff meeting at Colorado: I made 22 suggestions, and not one of them was taken seriously, let alone taken. I knew where I stood right away. And then I began to find out how much I didn't know about football, particularly the X's and O's.

I was embarrassed, really, and I often stayed at the office until midnight by myself learning what I needed to learn. Eventually, I caught on. I came to understand why the 22 suggestions hadn't been worth a darn.

One thing I did know reasonably well, or so I thought, was how to recruit. When I was at Air Academy, I had seven of my kids go to Missouri and a number of others were recruited. I had college coaches in my office every spring and fall, and I went on every home visit when recruiters came in. I listened carefully to how they approached the players, and I learned a lot about what worked and didn't work. I had begun applying that at Fort Lewis.

But I made a couple of humongous mistakes early on in recruiting for Colorado, when part of my territory was Wichita, Kansas. A coach at one of the schools there had told me about this defensive lineman who was 6' 5", 265 pounds. At the time we were craving defensive linemen. Over at Wichita North, there was a running back named Sanders who sounded like he was too little to play. When Mac was asking his assistants who we liked in our territories, I told him about this defensive lineman—who I'd never seen—and that he was going to be a great player.

Well, a couple weeks later I went back to the school and finally saw some film of this guy. I asked the coach, "Hey, how big did you say he was?" And he said, "6' 3", 235." I thought, "Really? Well, he'll have to get bigger, but that's probably still big enough."

The first day you could see kids was December 1, and I rented a car in Wichita and drove over to this kid's house. He lived in a trailer, and he came to the door and looked me in the eye: I'm barely 6' 1", so he was maybe 6 feet. And he was wearing some kind of brace on his leg. All I could think was, "Oh, no, Mac will fire me if I bring this kid back as my top recruit for the defensive line." I had no idea what to do, so I hemmed and hawed. I was supposed to go see the Sanders kid the next night, but I felt so foolish I just got out of Wichita and never went back.

Well, Barry Sanders went on to have a decent career at Oklahoma State—which might have been the only school he visited. Just sort of lucked into the ol' Heisman Trophy. As for the lineman, I wrote him a note and said that we had already committed to some other linemen. We had, so I didn't flat-out lie to him, but I felt bad about the whole deal.

Because of that experience, I will never recruit another player without at least seeing him in a school hallway to know how big he is. Most kids are misrepresented at least a little in terms of size and speed; it's not usually done on purpose, but that's the way it is.

The 1984 season was my first at CU and Mac's third, and it was a disaster. We went 1–10, and everybody killed us—when we didn't kill ourselves. We missed four field goals against Michigan State, and we got shellacked by Notre Dame and UCLA.

It was a miserable environment. It really looked like we were going to be fired, but for some reason the administration kept us. In retrospect, I'd have to call that belief without evidence.

I watched Mac closely during that season, especially the way he led and motivated. He was strong, brilliant. We still were dealing mostly with players he had inherited, but you could see the quality and promise of the young players he had recruited. It was important for me, too, that I got to see him make mistakes and recover from them.

We had a lot of struggles as a staff in the off-season. Some positions had opened and Mac wanted to bring in people that the rest of us didn't feel good about. We had a lot of arguments, but Mac eventually listened to us. It was a hard time, but it was a tremendous learning experience.

We changed the offense for the next season to the Wishbone. Mac would change offenses at the drop of a hat, and one of the things he later advised me to do was to find a system and stick with it.

In our first scrimmage with the Wishbone we fumbled 23 times. In the second, we fumbled 13 times. In the third, it was down to seven and by the spring game, we fumbled just once.

We tidied up the offense enough to win seven games in 1985 and go to the Freedom Bowl. That was a glorious day. We had saved our jobs, and we were able to recruit much better after that.

Sometimes, it seemed like Mac willed everything into success.

No matter what anybody thinks about Mac—and he was criticized plenty for voicing his passionate religious beliefs—he is a man of amazing convictions about what he does. When he has a conviction, he does everything 100 mph, and you don't just get a piece of Mac—you get all of Mac. The rest of us might not have the courage or the energy to pursue things like he does, but he has both in abundance.

He is the definition of single-mindedness and purpose. He was like a racehorse with built-in blinders—he couldn't see anything but the end of the track. He was a stickler for detail, and he really knew what he was doing.

Mac's management style, especially early on, was to create crises and stir the pot up. That was his way of creating opportunities for us to solve problems and be inventive. At times those who worked for him thought he was an absolute tyrant or nuts—but he was always fair, and we all would have fought for him.

Most of the first few years, though, we just fought him. I was talking to Gerry DiNardo recently, and he reminded me that every day in our staff room came down to a fight. It was like if you weren't fighting, you weren't coaching. When Mac rejected my 22 suggestions, those weren't suggestions to him. Those were 22 fights.

For a while, we all just thought that was the way coaching was, but you don't have to do it that way. Eventually, that wasn't coaching to me. I just think that's what Mac had learned at Michigan under Bo Schembechler, who obviously had enormous success. I think when Mac grew out of that and became Bill McCartney instead of an extension of Bo Schembechler, he was the best coach in the country.

As competitive as Mac is, he also is one of the most compassionate people I've ever known. And no one was more eloquent. He has a mastery of the English language, and he can speak with evangelical power. I've never seen anyone who could talk to players the way he could. He could bring them to tears like *that*.

Among the traits of his that I've tried to emulate are attention to detail and abrupt, confrontational honesty. He always said, "People can deal with the truth. When you hide the truth, that's what they can't handle. They won't forgive you for hiding the truth, but they can deal with hearing the truth."

A simple example of something we do at Northwestern because of Mac is the way we travel. When we fly, I always put our seniors in first class, just like we did at Colorado. When I came to Northwestern and requested that, the administration wouldn't let me do it. They said they thought it was more appropriate for administrators and their guests.

After an administrative change, though, we were able to do it. I think it shows the degree of priority we give our seniors, and I like it when people board a plane and see what kind of guys our seniors are. It seems like a good way to expose something I'm very proud of.

We lost our first four games at Colorado in 1986, but then, for the first time in 20 years, we beat Nebraska—which Mac had red-lettered on our schedule to foster a rivalry—and we went 6–1 in the Big Eight and played in the Bluebonnet Bowl. We qualified for a bowl again in 1987, but our administration was upset with Mac and wouldn't let us go.

Between the '86 and '87 seasons, Mac had been offered the Southern Methodist job and, really, had decided to take it. That in turn created a rift in our staff because he could only take five of us. In any case, the administration assumed Mac was gone, but at the last minute Mac pulled out and we all stayed.

But by the time he walked back into that building, we felt that Colorado already had us emotionally replaced. They didn't want us there. I was absorbing the whole scene and learning how administrations functioned. Still, the Colorado program by now had momentum. We went to the 1988 Freedom Bowl—after the season opened with a jarring scare for our family.

Clay was 11 then, and I was pushing for him to be a ballboy during our opening game with Fresno State. When we were leaving the house, Mary said, "Are you sure he's old enough to do this?" I said, "Absolutely." We had two sets of three ballboys working, one on each sideline. I wasn't sure which sideline Clay and his two buddies were on.

In the third quarter, one of our running backs, J.J. Flannigan, crashed out of bounds on the other side of Folsom Field, which doesn't have a lot of sideline room. It took a long time for everyone to unpile, and the official called timeout. Then one ref came over and said, "We've got a ballboy who doesn't have any vital signs over there."

I hadn't seen Clay all game, and I frantically looked down our sideline to see if he was there. I saw the other group of three kids, so I immediately knew Clay was on the other side. I was on the headset with Mac, and I said, "Mac, I've got to go over there" and ran to the other side of the field. I knew Clay was wearing sneakers with orange circles on the bottoms—and as I got over to the pileup I could see the orange circles. I waved to Mary, and she took right off down 40 steep steps.

Clay, as it turned out, was coming to; I don't know what that stuff about vital signs was about. But he had suffered a compound fracture of the arm, and the ambulance came out on the field to take him to the hospital. Mary went in the ambulance, and I left the game early and went over, too. They had to re-break his arm to set it.

Mary was pretty upset with me, and I had to sleep on the couch for about two weeks after that. But, hey, as a result the Big Eight passed what I call the Clay Barnett Rule: You have to be 18 to be a ballboy.

Sal Aunese was our quarterback that season, but in the spring of 1989 he was diagnosed with stomach cancer.

Sal had a magnetic presence, a charisma about him. Everybody wanted to be around him, and he lifted up anybody who was. He led in a more natural way than anybody I've ever known. He didn't always make good decisions off the field, but he was a good person and ran our offense exceptionally.

Before our first game that fall, I took all the quarterbacks and fullbacks over to see Sal. He had been undergoing chemotherapy, and his skin was blackened. It was a heartbreaking sight.

His illness was one of the most emotional battles I've ever gone through, in coaching or otherwise. Sal became our cause that year and, really, the next. The kids wanted Sal on their brain. They wanted him all around us. They wanted his jersey in the locker room, so we put it and his equipment behind plexiglass in a locker. He watched our games from the press level, and the kids pointed up to him after games.

Then they pointed to the sky after he died early in the season.

I remember people accusing us of manipulating the situation, and I took great offense to that. But I'm sure people on the outside just couldn't understand what we were going through.

We went 11–1 that season and lost the national championship game to Notre Dame 21–6 in the Orange Bowl.

To me, one of the critical issues of 1989 had been our team captains standing up and taking control of things, such as not letting players party during the week.

The captains let it be known that this was the way it was going to be, and it needed to come from them. This may seem minor, but I don't believe you can minimize the significance of chemistry and singlemindedness of purpose.

Their decision not to party during the week stemmed from a rash of arrests that had plagued the team during the mid-'80s. A number of those arrests involved black athletes. To the black athlete, Boulder was a very safe place from a life-and-death standpoint. But with a black population of just two percent, it could be a very scary, sometimes hostile, place from a cultural sensitivity standpoint.

There were times we felt like our kids were being mistreated by the campus and Boulder police, and I think that was part of the reason we had a few streaks of arrests. It got reported that it was like an epidemic, but I think that was blown out of proportion. It's true there were quite a few arrests over a three- or four-year period, and several of them were very serious matters. But many of the arrests were the direct result of bar fights and racial slurs; they were certainly nothing to be condoned but neither were they felonies. I think there were some perceptions on the outside that we had consciously recruited thugs, but that was never the case and I don't think we had bad kids. I believe that perception began to change when we set up some seminars with a black psychologist named Will Miles and worked with Boulder and campus police to initiate a ride-along program with our players—so each party could become more aware of and sensitive to the other.

All of this, of course, was a great education for me, because I hadn't had much exposure to blacks in general, let alone the black athlete, and was initially concerned that I might not know how to relate to them.

This is another area where I borrowed generously from Mac: When I got to Northwestern, I had Dr. Ulysses "Duke" Jenkins, an assistant dean of students who works in African-American affairs, talk to our coaches. We too have a ride-along program, which lets the players see the dangers police have to face and enables the police to understand what our guys are about.

The predicament in 1990, though, was this: A rhythm and blues night had been established at a local nightspot for every Thursday. One of the longstanding issues in Boulder was that there were very few sources of entertainment for the black students. This new spot was going to be a place where all the black students could go and listen to music. About the only other options for that were a half hour away in Denver, and that drive wasn't something we wanted to encourage. But the fact that the local R&B night was on Thursdays was a real source of conflict for us, because until the captains took action in 1989, partying on Thursday nights in particular had been a problem.

When our seniors set out to make a decision in 1990 on how they were going to handle Thursday nights, the vote split along racial lines. I was in charge of the senior players and, therefore, the seniors who set policy. I had pressure on me from our other coaches to intervene and make the vote go one particular direction, but I didn't see that as my role. I saw my role as a facilitator, not an enforcer. The players voted to be able to go out on Thursdays, with the provision that they police themselves.

The aftermath wasn't real comfortable for me. Frankly, a couple of coaches thought I'd really let everybody down. I believe Mac felt that way, too.

We opened the 1990 season early, against Tennessee in the

71

Pigskin Classic. A couple of guys, including our running back, Eric Bieniemy, had gotten into a row with police in July and were suspended for the game. Our policy was that if you embarrass our team publicly, you're going to miss a game. We ended up tying 31–31, and if Tennessee had gone for a two-point conversion at the end of the game, our guys were so tired I'm sure Tennessee could have walked in.

Here we were, with all these great expectations, and we open up with a tie. The second game was with Stanford, and they completely surprised us with their defensive plan. Some unbelievable things had to happen for us to rally. We won 21–17 on the last play, a fourth and goal situation. Then we lost 23–22 to Illinois, which we had beaten like a drum the year before.

So we were 1-1-1, and our visions of a national championship seemed to be fading rapidly.

Meanwhile, a couple of our young black players had gotten into fights two Thursday nights in a row. Our kids had said they were going to police themselves on Thursdays, but they weren't doing the job. That issue was rearing its ugly head, and I was getting a lot of flak.

Finally, I called in Alfred Williams, one of our captains, and appealed to him to look at it objectively. Alfred is black, and he had the courage to say, "We're wrong. Thursday night is hurting the team. We're 1-1-1, and we're not what we could have been."

I don't know how many of the players actually held themselves to staying in on Thursdays, but they were accountable to each other now and we didn't have any more problems on Thursday nights. I sensed the tension ease, and I think that improved our chemistry immensely. I honestly believe the intangible of good chemistry may have accounted for what we went on to accomplish; at least it became one of the forces working with us.

We played at Texas next, and we came from behind, again, to win 29–22. Then we played Washington—it was a brutal nonconference schedule every year, but Mac loved that—and rallied to win that one 20–14 after quarterback Darian Hagan was hurt. Charles Johnson, a former walk-on, came in for Darian against Washington, and he was going to have to play the next week at Missouri, too.

Missouri's field was Omniturf, and there had been trouble with it ever since it was put in. Too much sand in the mix, or something like that. In warmups the morning of the game, our kids were slipping like crazy. And they were panicking. I looked over at Missouri, and the players weren't slipping at all. They must have had more appropriate footwear, longer cleats. We had a few pairs of longer ones, but not enough to go around.

When we came out, the first two times Charles ran the option he slipped. Just flat fell down. Every time we tried to cut, we were falling. Missouri was moving the ball on us like crazy.

At halftime, Mac came to me and said, "We're not playing C.J. anymore." I replied, "Mac, you can't do that." He said, "He's not a good enough athlete to play in this game. We've got to play Hagan."

So they gave Hagan a shot, a pain reliever, so he could play. I was real angry at Mac, as angry as I ever was at him, and I went over to C.J. to tell him what we were going to do.

C.J. just started crying. I said, "Now, look, we both know that Darian is hurt and can't play. You're going to have to go back in and win this game. You've got to get over this feeling; you can't let this stand in the way of what's going to happen."

In the third quarter Darian ran two plays, slipped both times, aggravated his shoulder and came back out. So Mac said, "Put C.J. back in."

Late in the second half, with maybe two minutes left, we were trailing 31–27 and got the ball deep in our territory. We started to drive, and Bieniemy had a clear lane to the end zone at one point only to slip. Again. Mac was screaming, but there wasn't anything we could do. With 31 seconds left, though, we had a first down on the Missouri three-yard line.

We only had one timeout left, so when we got to the line of scrimmage we ran what's called a "speedy"—where the quarterback immediately spikes the ball in the dirt to stop the clock.

Meanwhile, the Missouri sideline was going crazy trying to get their goal line defense set, and their coaches were trying to call timeout. Almost simultaneously, I guess, we snapped the ball and threw it in the dirt. The clock stopped, but we couldn't quite tell what happened.

On our sideline, we didn't know Missouri had been assessed a timeout and initially thought we would be charged with a down. I asked C.J. what happened, and he said Missouri called timeout before we threw the ball. I said, "Are you sure?" and our center, Jay Leeuwenburg said, "Yeah, that's what the ref told us." I looked over on the scoreboard, and sure enough there was "1" on there and "1" on the chains.

So we didn't give that play another thought; it was never a consideration that that play would count. The Missouri people,

73

though, must have thought we had gotten the play off before the timeout was called.

We stayed in our first-down mode, then. We ran a play, and they stopped us, and we used our timeout. Mac called the official over and said, "We're going to run another running play, and then we're going to throw another speedy. Don't let them hold us down while the clock's running." Like clockwork, we ran another play and didn't get in, and Missouri held our kids down. The officials blew the whistle to give us time to line up, and we threw the speedy and stopped the clock.

Now there were about two seconds left, and it was fourth down from less than a yard away. C.J. took the ball and spun toward the end zone. It took a while, but the officials signaled touchdown—and we won 33–31.

Of course, we just went crazy. It was an incredible win. But then we started hearing that people in the stands and in the press box were saying we had used five downs. By the time we tried to leave the field, bottles, cans, everything was coming at us. Hagan gave me his flak jacket to wear over my head.

We got in the locker room, and Mac came over and said, "What's this five downs they're talking about?" I explained to him what had happened, and he said, "Alright." Very few people really know the story, but if we had thought that a down had been used I don't think we would have spiked the ball on fourth down just to see if we could get away with it. We deserve a bit more credit than that.

When Mac met the press, he said the story of the game wasn't the "five downs"—it was the condition of the field. That made the Missouri people furious. When we went back through the film, though, we counted something like 99 slips by our players.

Mac is also a Missouri graduate, and the whole situation caused a controversy. People there couldn't believe we didn't try to give them the game back. It was a real stink, and things like that don't die in Missouri. To be honest, if I still had been a Boy Scout from Mexico, Missouri, I'm sure I would have gone nuts about it myself. If I'd had something to throw, I probably would have, too.

What we later put on our national championship rings was, "The Will to Win." We had to come from behind, I believe, in 10 of 13 games that year. Some people had portrayed us as remarkably lucky, but I find it hard to accept that it's luck if you do it over and over again with all the adversity we faced.

Just to make sure we expressed ourselves on the issue, we beat

Missouri 55–7 at Folsom Field the next year. For all the commotion Mizzou had made about "the Fifth Down," I have to admit it was soothing to look up and see the two 5s on our side of the scoreboard. I wouldn't say we ran up the score, but I think we scored what needed to be scored.

After the so-called Fifth-Down Game, the game I really remember that season was Nebraska. It was about 30 degrees, and the rain was falling horizontally. We fell a couple touchdowns behind—what else was new? But Bieniemy scored four times in the fourth quarter, and we won the Big Eight championship again. A number of other circumstances fell our way and set us up for another chance at the national championship against Notre Dame.

In the weeks before the Orange Bowl, Gerry DiNardo, our offensive coordinator, told Mac he was leaving before the game to take the Vanderbilt job. Much the way he interviewed me to come to Colorado, Mac approached me and said, "You're going to be the offensive coordinator for the national championship game. You'll do fine."

No, I didn't throw up.

I set about doing it my way, and Mac was incredible. Not one time did he insist on making suggestions, not one time did he insist something couldn't be done. He just let me take it and run with it, and I think that influenced how I try to handle my staff.

I recall that game so vividly. Everything moved so fast. I had memorized the game plan, and I called almost the whole game without wearing a headset. I knew just what I wanted to do.

We were leading 10–9 late in the game when a lot of people got a real scare, or thrill, on Rocket Ismail's apparent punt return for a touchdown. But I was okay about it because I had seen an official throw a penalty flag for clipping. The play came back, Deon Figures intercepted for us a couple plays later—and we were national champions.

Right after the game, I stood back and let it all wash over me and watched everybody celebrate. I just wanted to see everybody have a heck of a time. I was exhausted and mostly relieved.

When we got back to our hotel on the beach that night, we went up on the roof for a party for coaches and friends. I remember looking out in the open air, just thinking, "Wow."

8.

The Lunge of Faith

*"We are continually faced by great
opportunities brilliantly disguised as insoluble problems."*
—Lee Iacocca

My last season in Colorado was 1991. We didn't win the national
championship again—we were 8-2-1—but it might have been the
best coaching I ever did.

We had lost a lot of players and had a lot of turbulence with
staff turnover, but we really put together what we had. Probably
the most satisfying moments came in our win at Oklahoma,
where we had two textbook, length-of-the-field drives. On the
plane coming back, Mac turned toward me and said, "Barney—
two 99-yard drives in one game? I've never seen that."

In Mac's own way, I think that was probably the highest compliment he ever gave me. That was how I took it, anyway.

By late fall, Mary and I had had a house built with a breath-
taking, 180-degree view of the mountains. We had a creek running through our backyard, and Mary planted all these flowers.
It was really a nice home, and we had just gotten a great deal with
this golf course. I was getting a new Lincoln Continental every
six months, recruiting was really humming, and I had a brand
new office overlooking the field.

Mac had a lifetime contract, so I could probably stay at Colorado as long as I wanted. We had close friends that we loved to
be around. We kind of had life by the tail. I mean, life was pretty
danged good.

As an assistant coach, you never really know when people in
other parts of the country are talking about you—and you certainly never feel like they are.

So it was funny when I came to Northwestern, because a number of newspaper people asked me, "You were such a high-pro-

file guy—why would you take the Northwestern job?" Well, I certainly didn't think I was "high-profile," and I had no idea that I was considered that way. I think maybe people in Missouri knew my name a little, but if you asked somebody in California I'm sure they wouldn't have known who I was.

Besides not feeling particularly coveted, I was in no way anxious to look for a job. The only one I ever really thought about was Missouri, and I couldn't even get an interview there when it came open in 1988—or in 1993, for that matter.

The Tuesday before Thanksgiving, 1991, I was out with John Wristen, a graduate assistant coach, getting new tires on my car. Over the radio we heard that Francis Peay had been fired at Northwestern. It zinged me, for some reason. I turned to John and said, "You know, that's a job I might be able to get."

Back at the office, I told Mac that Francis had been fired. He said, "Is that right? Want me to make a call?" The president of Northwestern, Arnold Weber, had hired Mac at Colorado, and Bill Fischer, formerly a vice-president of finance at Colorado, had become VP of finance at Northwestern.

I went home that night and said, "Guess what? Northwestern opened up today." Mary asked, "Well, what's that mean?" I said I didn't know what it meant. Courtney said, "Cool, dad! That's where I want to go to school." We could have sent Courtney to Colorado, but we couldn't have afforded to send her to Northwestern. Keep in mind that I didn't make $40,000 until after I was 40 years old.

We drove to Nevada, Missouri, for Thanksgiving and kicked the idea around a little more on the trip, but nobody really seemed to think much about it. When we arrived, though, I found out there was a message at home from Bill Carr, a head-hunter for Northwestern.

He had talked to Mac and was calling to set up a phone interview. I went over to see my mom in Mexico and she said, "Oh, you shouldn't go to Northwestern. They're just terrible." She called cousins of mine in Illinois, and they said, "That's a terrible job. You don't ever want to do that."

Well, I did the phone interview with Bill Carr on Sunday night, and now Northwestern was going to fly me out for a meeting at the Hyatt near O'Hare Field. The juices started flowing a little bit. A lot. Mac reminded me that I was in a position of strength and that I should go through the process.

Of course, it was well-documented how bad the program had been. But Mac pointed out that I was on the good side of the two most important people: the president and the guy in charge of the money. He also said, "Your quality of life changes as a head coach."

Northwestern initially brought in four or five other guys, too; the other finalists were Earle Bruce, Paul Schudel and Gary Darnell. They asked me, and I assume all of us, to put together some philosophical material and a plan for the first six months, things like that.

Whether I got the job or not, it was really a good exercise for me to do. I'd say I've refined some of my thoughts since, but much of what I submitted then still has great meaning for me:

I. PHILOSOPHY
  A. General
    1. My family comes first.
    2. Never accept second place.
    3. Teach, drive, motivate, mold to perfection.
    4. Compete every day.
    5. Do everything with class.
    6. Never be intimidated by anyone.
    7. Be a little unconventional.
  B. Leadership
    1. Perceptiveness is the secret. (Calm in crisis, positive thinking).
    2. First mark of a leader is a man who can lead himself.
      a. Wisdom to plan.
      b. Courage to act.
      c. Capability to manage.
  C. Football
    1. Football teaches that we need each other.
    2. Two types of education: one teaches us how to make a living, the other teaches us how to live.
    3. Attitude and chemistry are the factors that control the levels of winning, no matter what the talent level.
    4. Win and graduate.

II. PROGRAM GOALS
  A. Graduate student-athletes.
    1. Turn potential into productivity.
    2. Athletes are first. Never ask them to do anything bad for themselves.
    3. Ask our players to hold themselves responsible for a higher standard than others expect of them.

B. Teach the key ingredients for success.
1. Team morale comes first.
2. Ability to adjust. Overcome adversities.
3. Worry about the elements we can control.
4. Establish the will to succeed.
5. Decide who we are, where we are going and how we are going to get there.
C. Win football games.
1. Out-motivate, out-communicate, outwork, and out-recruit our opponents.
2. When we win, there will be enough glory for everyone.
3. Preparation + confidence + character = success.
4. Consistency.
D. Get to a postseason bowl.

III. RECRUITING
A. Recruit character.
1. Is he committed to excellence?
2. Can I trust him?
3. Does he care about others?
B. Don't worry about the ones who get away; it's the ones you take that can't play that defeat you.
C. There is an abundance of good student-athletes in this country. Don't sell America's youth short.

I also did a complete section on academics, mostly pointing out how we handled study tables, mentor programs and the like at Colorado. In a section called "Non-Conference Schedule," I wrote that I would work with the athletic director to create the most competitive schedule possible. "Most people shoot too low and hit rather than too high and miss," I added. Under "December" in the first 12-month calendar, I included "bowl season and preparation." I also had sections on discipline—"the foundation of all successful teaching and coaching,"—style of play, and, most important, selecting assistant coaches.

The outline stimulated me but I wouldn't say I was obsessed with the job. It wasn't anything I had to have. When they asked me after the interview if I wanted to continue in the process, it was like, "Hey, sure. Why not?"

At that point, though, I started feeling a little more tugged. One of my problems is that if you put something out in front of me as a challenge I tend to go for it whether it makes sense or not, whether I need it or not. I don't know if I really wanted to continue in the process, but I couldn't say no. I started thinking about who else was involved, and it started becoming a competition: "Who do I have to beat out?" Without saying it aloud, that was what I was thinking.

Still, I was pretty skeptical. Mac asked me what I thought, and I said the schedule was ridiculous for a team that needed to rebuild and mentioned how Northwestern opened up with Notre Dame the next four years. That wasn't a good deal. I'm like Mac in wanting to play the big powers, but you have to have a base under you first.

Then Northwestern called me back and said I was one of a few finalists. They flew Mary and me out, and we met a group for dinner. It was a dreary and wet night, and as we talked to everybody it became apparent to me that no one had any idea about what it took to have a winning college football program. When Mary and I went up to our hotel room later, she said, "They don't have a clue, do they?"

It seemed incredible, but none of them had ever been a part of a winning team. If you haven't seen it done, of course, there's no way you can understand what it takes to pave the way to having it done. And these were the people who were going to have to pave the way!

They were asking me questions about how I was going to cut spending—when Northwestern already was light years behind the other budgets in the Big Ten. I was told, for example, that it was abusive to spend money on taking players to a hotel the night before home games. Well, to me it's just not sensible to do anything else, because of all the temptations and noise around dormitories on Friday nights.

I did think Dyche Stadium was neat, and Bruce Corrie, the athletic director, took me up into the creaky old press box. I mean, it's antiquated. When we got up there, somebody turned the power off and the elevator off and we were stuck for almost an hour. It was freezing, and there was no way down. We finally got out by crawling through a side window.

Maybe the power being turned off in the stadium was a good metaphor for the whole interview experience. I never felt any energy on campus in any way for football. On the flight back, Mary said, "You aren't going to take this job, are you?" I said, "No, I'm not going to take it." Then she asked, "Are you interested?" I said,

81

"I don't know. I shouldn't be, but there is a little interest. But I'm not going to take it."

I spent the next week helping Colorado prepare for Alabama in the Blockbuster Bowl, and Mac now wanted to change the offense to a one-back set. Mac asked how it went at Northwestern and if I thought I would get offered the job. I told him I thought I would but that I wasn't going to take it.

Mac talked again about what an ally Arnold Weber, the president of Northwestern, had been to the Colorado program and how overnight my financial world would change and that I'd be able to send Courtney to Northwestern. If this works out, he told me, all of my coaches would be in total demand—and so would I. Then he said, "You know, if you do this for five years and it doesn't work out, you can come back here." But he cautioned me not to take it unless I met with Arnie and got everything up front that I needed to get the program moving.

I was out recruiting Matt Russell in Illinois, and I told him there was a possibility I would be leaving for Northwestern. When I left, Mary called on the car phone to say Northwestern had called and offered me the job. I called Bruce and told him I wasn't interested unless I could have a private meeting first with Arnie Weber.

That was arranged for the next day, and that night I talked to a few people, including: Bill Tobin, another Missouri guy who was close to Francis; Lou Tepper, a former colleague at Colorado and now Illinois' coach; and Gerry DiNardo. I tried calling Francis at one point during all this, but we never connected.

Bill thought I should wait for the Missouri job to open. Lou thought the situation might be okay but that the schedule was atrocious (I agreed, but I also didn't want to flinch at the schedule; so since I didn't know what to say, I never brought it up). Gerry really wondered. The consensus was I shouldn't take the job.

Before I met with Arnie the next morning, I met with Corrie and Fischer and they outlined the terms of the contract. They said, "Is this okay?"

I had been told never to go into a negotiation like this without an agent or lawyer, but I didn't have an agent or lawyer. This was really the first time I'd dealt with a contract, and I felt like I was at their mercy. I mean, they had me. But I managed to say, "That's not enough money." They told me I'd have to take that up with Arnie.

So I went in to Arnie and he said, "I assume that the contract looked okay?" I said, "No. Between Mary and me we're already making this much, and this job is potentially coaching suicide. I'm going to have to have more." I mentioned that Mary was part of the deal, that she was probably going to work as hard and spend as much time on this as I was, so they weren't going to be getting just one person.

Arnie was an old labor negotiator, so he agreed to more money and other items—but put in the contract that if Mary went back to work I'd have to pay back some of the money they were paying me.

We talked some more and he said, "Now, do we have a deal?" I said I needed an hour to talk and think it over. I called home; Mary and I had kept Courtney and Clay home from school so we could all talk about it. We talked for about 59 minutes and then Courtney said, "Dad, let's go for it!" And Clay said, "No, no, no."

When I hung up I didn't know what I was going to do. I knew Bruce Corrie was waiting outside, and I had no idea what I was going to say as I took the elevator down and went outside to his car.

I walked out and put my hand on the door latch, pulled it out and opened the door—and I still didn't know what I was going to say. I had no idea what was going to come out of my mouth.

Then I said, "Looks like you've got yourself a coach."

9.

Tollways

*"There are two days in every week about which
we should not worry; two days which should be kept from
fear and apprehension. One of these days is yesterday, with
its mistakes and cares.... The other day we
should not worry about is tomorrow, with its possible
burdens.... That leaves only one day—Today! Any man can
fight the battle of just one day. It is only when
you and I carry the burdens of those two awful eternities—
yesterday and tomorrow—that we break down."*
—Anonymous

My next words to Bruce Corrie after accepting the Northwestern job were, "We've got some work to do."

As much as I respect Francis Peay, I knew I wasn't replacing a legend and that the program had nowhere to go but up. But I had no idea how bad the decay was. I was really naive about Northwestern.

For that matter I still was fairly naive in a more general sense. A few months after I got the job I made my first substantial visit to New York City to see a couple of major boosters. I'd never been on Fifth Avenue before, and I felt a little like the character on the show *McCloud*, who is something of a hick.

Every time a taxi honked, I thought it was honking at me. At one point, I was walking along a sidewalk admiring a building—it turned out to be Trump Tower—and I looked around and it seemed like about 15 people were just staring at me.

All of a sudden, this black limo pulls up along the curb and a policeman jumps out and pushes me to the side. Who gets out of the limo but Mikhail Gorbachev. He walked right over to me and shook my hand. He said, "Hello, nice to meet you," then disappeared into the building.

* * *

We announced my hiring at a press conference the day after I made my decision, and I said we would be extremely well-coached, well-conditioned and would always expect victory. I also said that grass does not grow under my feet and that I would begin recruiting immediately.

A few weeks later I was jogging with Tom Boeh, the associate athletic director for external affairs, and I told him I was trying to decide on a slogan. He said, "You know, what you said in the press conference was perfect."

I said, "You mean, 'Expect victory'?" And that was it. After we came out with that, a few people had some fun with how ridiculous it sounded. But I never wavered from that thought.

I told Mac I'd like to coach in the Blockbuster Bowl with the Colorado team, but he told me to get to work for Northwestern. Still, I flew down to Florida for the game, watched from the press box—a weird feeling—and flew back. Some of my new assistants and their wives came back with me, and we celebrated New Year's Eve in my office with some pizzas. Then we started to work.

I'd been a head coach before, of course, but the responsibility and magnitude of the jobs at the Air Academy and Fort Lewis were not remotely like this. It was like the difference between the universe and a planet, especially in a situation such as Northwestern's. It was like, "Where do I start?"

In jigsaw management, when there is utter chaos, the only way to cope is by setting priorities. You have to process all the information that comes to you, and you've got to sort out what's important and what isn't and deal later with what you deem less important. I had to complete a staff, and I had to recruit. Absolutely everything else had to wait.

I'm not hung up on hierarchy, and I know nothing was more crucial to the makeover of this football program than our assistant coaches. I wanted to have great teachers, I wanted them to feel like they worked with me, not for me, and I wanted this to be a hard place to leave.

Just as I've said about our players, every coach deserves a head coach who believes in him. If I hired them, they're mine and I believe in them. They would have to commit a felony before I would get rid of them.

Every year I've told our coaches, "We are the difference-makers. We have to turn over every rock, every stone, and put our finger in every dike. The way we're going to make up the difference in talent is coaching. We are as good or better than the people we coach against."

Our overall attitude and chemistry began with the staff, and I think we have a unique and exciting combination of experience and character. All of my assistant coaches are charismatic, and I sincerely believe each will be a head coach if he wants to be:

Greg Meyer, offensive coordinator—The two toughest positions to coach on any staff are the position that the head coach used to hold and the coordinator's job on the side of the ball that the head coach used to oversee. So Greg and Craig Johnson, our quarterbacks coach, have it the roughest.

Greg may be the nicest man I've ever known. He's tremendously organized, extremely thorough and has a great spirit about him. He also really knows how to handle me well; he lets me get upset and vent, and then he stands up for himself and what's right.

Greg came to us from Toledo, but we go back to my high school days in Colorado when he was coaching nearby.

Craig Johnson, quarterbacks—I've known Craig since his playing days in Colorado and at Wyoming. He came to us from the Virginia Military Institute and is a superb blend of organization and class. He was a military brat, and everything for Craig is extremely organized and clear-cut. He is a great role model for our black athletes.

Tom Brattan, offensive line—Tom is the consummate line coach, and no positions on the field other than defensive backs require more vigorous coaching. There are only a few guys in the country who can coach all five line positions effectively, and Tom is one of those few.

Tom, who joined us from William & Mary, had been a longtime high school coach, and he loves kids. He lives and dies with his linemen.

Gregg Brandon, receivers—Gregg played for me at Air Academy High School, and he was in the class where I created havoc with my interpretation of John Carlos and Tommie Smith's actions at the 1968 Olympics. He's extremely loyal and gets more things done in a day than any coach I know—great time-management skills. He's also very knowledgeable about the game.

John Wristen, running backs—There isn't anybody who doesn't like John. He's got a tremendous knack for recruiting, and he's got a real feel for ongoing game adjustments. That's a rare quality, because when the guns are blazing during a game not everyone can be composed enough or focused enough to understand the big picture. He sees that, but he can also narrow down what's important.

Ron Vanderlinden, defensive coordinator—Ron is very dynamic, and he's blossomed into one of the bright young minds in college football right now. I came to know his capabilities—and we really became close friends—during our eight years together at Colorado. Now, I just let Ron create. He has total freedom.

Jerry Brown, defensive backs—Jerry is a Northwestern graduate and one of the finest teachers and greatest people I've ever been around. He represents a true father figure. From his demeanor, I knew the minute he walked in my office that he was the guy for the job. Jerry's experience as an assistant coach with the Minnesota Vikings helped give him the credibility and expertise that is needed to coach these vital positions.

Tim Kish, outside linebackers—We have to take the coffee away from Tim. He has an unbelievable surplus of energy and enthusiasm. He exudes excitement, and he's a spark not only for our players but also our staff. His spirit is contagious. The players love him, but he drives them.

Vince Okruch, defensive line—Vince is hard-nosed and demanding and accepts nothing but perfection in anything he does. The players really respond to him and respect him. He's organized but very creative, particularly when it comes to recruiting. He has the ability to sense what the 17- and 18-year olds are thinking or could be affected by.

In addition to our full-time, on-field staff, Jeff Genyk is our program coordinator—and the next coaching opening I have will go to him. He has great administrative skills and could probably be an athletic director right now. His background was in the business world, where he was driving a Porsche and making six figures before he decided he wanted to coach.

Jeff came here as a graduate assistant, a position currently filled by Matt Limegrover, who is very bright, and David Hansburg, who has a creative flair. At one point during the search process, David sent me a cellular phone in the mail with a note saying, "I'm sitting here waiting ... Here's the phone ... You make the call."

What David didn't know was, yes, we get a lot of applications for the G.A. jobs. But applicants first have to be accepted by Northwestern on their own, and Matt and David were the only two who got in out of the 100 applicants we had. I'm sure I would have called David anyway.

As intent as I was on keeping my staff intact, I knew I had to take measures to make it happen. I go to work every day wondering what I can do to make things better for the staff.

The first two raises that came through for them were disappointing, so I put my own raise into a pool for them. Nobody knew it except the athletic director and the people who handle the money. That didn't matter. What matters is that, as of this writing, we've had incredible continuity: two staff changes in five years.

The May after I was hired, Mike DeBord told me he was leaving for Michigan. Boy, was I angry. *Obsessive. Rage*, I later wrote in my journal. I was angry because I considered his move a reflection on me.

I had promised our kids I was bringing them coaches who would stay here, and they all had committed for two years. The kids had had enough of guys who didn't want to be here. I was fortunate to be able to bring in Tom Brattan then, but Mike's departure stuck with me for a long time.

The only other coaching change I've had to make was after the first season. The one coach I had kept from Francis' staff was Kevin Ramsey, because he was sharp and I wanted a black coach who could help with existing team members. Some of the other guys really wanted to stay, and I had nothing against them, but you've got to have your own people. I understood why Kevin left for another job, at West Virginia, but I still was hurt and in retrospect probably wouldn't have hired him if I had known he would leave.

But I never felt like Kevin really locked arms with the rest of us, and I was really pleased to be able to then hire Jerry Brown.

Among the things I've tried to do to keep the staff happy is to make Northwestern a place where they have freedom to create and a place where they could have input and ownership.

One thing I instituted to facilitate that is "Idea Days." Every coach gets an opportunity to present an idea that we will carry through. I mean, I'll still use the phrase that they're sick of— "Show me empirical data"—but they get 15-20 minutes to explain the concept, and a followup discussion of their idea. Maybe this practice comes from the 22 suggestions that went unused in my first meeting at Colorado.

Idea Days have only two rules. Nobody can respond to a presentation by going, "Yeah, but ..." And you can't say, "The problem with that idea is ..."

We want to try to make the idea work. We try every one of them, and their scope goes from ways to make our recruiting better to on-the-field matters to changes in our players' handbooks. Everything. Anything. Then I work with Jeff Genyk on providing the energy and resources to implement all the ideas.

If an idea doesn't work, that's valuable information, too. If you try it, you find out what works and doesn't work. If you don't try it, the idea just sort of sits back there and you always wonder if it would have worked. And if you never get a chance to express the ideas, that creates resentment.

We don't care who gets the credit. The problem would be *not* coming up with the ideas. Football is a game of changes. The dynamics are constantly in flux. You've got to be flexible, and this is a way for us to stay that way.

We're not operating under a mentality of, "If it ain't broke, don't fix it." We're going to break everything down and rebuild it every year. It's "What can we make better than what we had?"

If I don't wear certain clothes at home in a year's time, I give them away—even if it was a shirt I thought was pretty great when I bought it. Now, if I could get Mary to do the same thing ... The point is, just because we've always done something one way doesn't mean it's the right way, or that it has to stay that way.

It's in the same spirit of fostering ideas that I had grease boards installed in our coaches' bathrooms. When you're in there, it's like when you're shaving or running: You're doing something unconscious, and, for me, that's when I'm most creative. There have been times when I've been in there and thought, "This is a great idea—I've got to write this down." So now there's a place to write it down.

As crucial as it was to get the right staff together, the most obvious task was getting players. We had a window of one month to

90

accomplish what everybody else had been working toward for 11 months. We began with a list of names that had been compiled by Rob Chiavetta, the incumbent recruiting coordinator.

Well, there wasn't any way we could win the Big Ten with what I saw on film of those prospects, and I wasn't willing to settle for that. So we pored through films, trying to find guys we thought could at least come close to playing in the Big Ten. By that time of year, January, it was like trying to find needles in haystacks. We called those kids and almost every one of them had decided to go somewhere else or just wasn't interested in us.

But we persevered, and, along with guys we had been recruiting for Colorado, such as Shane Graham and William Bennett, we found a couple of local guys who were interested. Perhaps just as important, we promptly discovered what some of our local problems were:

Many area high school coaches felt disenfranchised by our program, so I assigned coaches as liaisons to each school and made plans for various clinics, camps and a summer "passing jamboree." Also, we had no idea of the geography of the Chicago area. One day I sent John Wristen out to visit kids at three different schools: Lake Forest, Oswego and Aurora. Well, it's a full day's driving just to get to all those sites, let alone conduct some business there, and you have to take toll roads.

Poor John, like the rest of us, had never been on the tollways here before and didn't have any change on him that day. He didn't know that if you ran out of money you were supposed to honk your horn and they'd raise the gate to let you through. So he had no idea what to do and got out of his car to check and people were cursing him and honking and ... what an experience.

Our first weekend of receiving recruiting visits provided my staff and me with our first chance to really see the campus. I remember being up on the second floor of the student union building, looking down on Lake Michigan and over to Chicago. Ron Vanderlinden just said, "Wow, what a beautiful campus. We can recruit here."

We knew we had a very valuable degree to offer, perhaps the best in Division I. We had a recruiting base of nearly eight million people a stone's throw away whereas in Colorado we had to fly all the way to California to recruit. The biggest single factor in recruiting still is proximity to home.

I looked down at the Lake Michigan beach and thought, "So

what if it's frozen over eight months a year? Nobody's got this to offer. Jeez, how could you not win?"

It wasn't long before we started finding out how we couldn't, about all the roadblocks and paper chases, but we still managed to keep our eyes on the mission immediately before us.

The first recruit to say yes to us was Justin Chabot, from Oxford, Ohio. His dad is the chairman of the English department of Miami of Ohio. Justin came on a visit with his parents that first recruiting weekend and on Sunday morning he said, "Coach, I want to be your first recruit." I said, "You're it!"

I'm not sure how many other schools we beat out on any of the guys we got, but we signed up a few we knew could play, and about seven of the eight we went for locally on our revised list. Those were significant investments in the future.

Of course all the recruiting gurus ranked our class the worst in the Big Ten, but it didn't make any difference to me. I was proud of that class, real proud, and I was going to believe in those guys from the minute we introduced them to the press until the time they graduated.

Recruiting is such a weird science, and it's so difficult for kids because they end up having so many good choices. The hardest part for them isn't saying yes. It's the three or four "no's" they have to give.

Ninety-nine percent of recruits say exactly the same thing when you ask them what they're looking for: I want to get a good education, I want a chance to play early, and I want to feel comfortable. In the end, most sign with schools that don't offer any of the three. So it's essential that you find out what really matters, which can be very difficult to do because there are so many possible factors. And kids often are taught by their high school coaches to mask their feelings.

As a recruiter, of course, it's also incredibly important that you be able to see through the mask to know what you might be getting. For example, is he an overachiever or an underachiever? One indicator we use for that is the grade-point average. If he's got a poor GPA, he may be an underachiever. It's very hard to take an underachiever and make him an overachiever. It can be done, but the percentages aren't with you.

Behavior is another consideration. There is a lot of pressure to bring in the blue-chip prospect, and you might choose not to hear everything that's being said about a spectacular player. If you're looking for this guy to be a great player who might make the difference for you, it's human nature to keep finding ways to validate that.

You don't ever purposely overlook character flaws. No coach I know of just recklessly says, "I've got a bad kid here, but I'm going to recruit him, anyway." But what happens is we can be influenced by their talent, and we tend to think that in our own setting we can make a difference and turn the kid around.

It's funny when you think about the whole situation. When a school sends out an acceptance letter to a general student, the school hasn't done nearly the amount of background checking that we do on a player. They don't go into their homes a half-dozen times, or even necessarily meet with them once.

Yet the college is willing to accept these students based purely on numbers and recommendations. So our players on the football team should be able to have a higher graduation and success rate than the general student, and I try to impress upon our kids that they should hold themselves to higher-than-average standards.

I believe that 85% of recruits have a good idea where they want to go before the process begins. If they haven't narrowed it down to the one school they want to go to, then at least they have it trimmed to their top three. What happens from there is that kids look to affirm their decision. There's just a small percentage whose minds you can change, or introduce a new idea to. But if they're not predisposed to listening to you, I don't think you're likely to get them.

There are exceptions, of course, and that's why you go after them anyway. You have to. But the most important skill you can have in recruiting is listening, so you can hear exactly what the athlete is saying and what it means.

Sometimes egos get involved and you feel like you can turn somebody around even though their mind is made up. Some-times—if it's not too cost-ineffective or too emotionally drain-ing—it's okay to try. But you can get emotionally involved, and it can be crushing to devote yourself to a recruit only to get jilted in the end. The best way to avoid being unpleasantly surprised—and the best way to enhance your position—is by figuring out who "the champion" is and getting whoever it is in your camp. "Champion" is a term we used at Colorado to describe who will be the most influential in the recruit's decision. It might not be one of his parents. Maybe it will be his girlfriend. Maybe it will be a coach. Or an uncle.

You have to know who that person is, though, because it's a

person who will champion your cause if you can win them over. And everybody has one.

After you determine what prospects you really have a chance with, genuineness, honesty, and caring are the most important things you can project. My role is to be a mentor, almost a parent, and I want the recruit's family to believe that I'm a man they want to have responsible for their son.

I have found the writings of a counseling psychologist named Carl Rogers to be instrumental. His basic theory states that in the relationship between the counselor and the client—not patient—trust influences behavior.

I became more or less a Rogerian in my counseling. It's not a foolproof theory. There are holes in it, and there are times you have to take other steps. But to produce trust requires sincerity, real empathy, which I think is critical in how you conduct yourself every day. And in recruiting.

When I was recruiting James Hill at Colorado, I told him I'd eat a steak the day he signed. Why? It was important for me not to eat red meat. So I wanted to tell him that I was willing to go against something that was pretty important to me if he would sign. I was trying to demonstrate how much I wanted him to come to Colorado. When he signed, well, I sat there in front of the media in Colorado Springs and ate a steak sandwich.

When I was recruiting Ray Robey, one of our defensive tackles at Northwestern, his father had recently hurt his foot in an accident at work. He was walking in a brace and couldn't wear a shoe. He was a very proud guy, and I could sense his self-consciousness, so I just took my shoes off.

I had no idea that was going to have any impact, but I was trying to create an atmosphere where Mr. Robey thought I cared and could trust me. I thought if I showed him I was sensitive to what he was going through that it would at least let him open up and talk. Ray later said my action was what triggered his decision to come here.

Ray also liked something else I'd said: that it's one thing to jump on a moving train and another to stop a train and turn it around. He wanted the challenge and adventure of turning Northwestern around, and we wanted people who wanted that.

Persistence also is a useful recruiting tool. I was on a recruiting swing through Florida with Tim Kish, who had gotten to know Chris Martin when Tim was recruiting for Army. Chris wasn't on our recruiting list, probably because he was short, but Tim and I were looking at somebody else at his high school and Tim thought I should meet Chris.

So we called Chris' house when we were there, and they said Chris was out but we could come over. We went and pitched Northwestern to Chris' mom, dad and dog. I didn't meet Chris until he made his recruiting visit here.

Once I addressed the immediate issues of hiring a staff and our first recruiting class, I was able to confront the rest of the chaos—beginning with the internal apathy and neglect and the team we took over. Everything had become so warped and self-defeating. It was one big Catch-22.

Our players were skipping weight-room workouts—and being backed by academic support on it. Kids weren't used to doing our type of workouts, didn't want to do that work, and they'd go to the academic support people, who would say, "Well, he has to spend more time on his studies." Instead of trying to manage their time better to be able to do both, some players were trying to find ways to get out of the hard part. That put academic support people in a bind, because they did not understand the significance of those workouts and assumed they would be detrimental to the academics.

Most of this pattern was circumstantial. It really wasn't anybody's fault. I mean, how could you blame the players?

Before my first meeting with them I went around the room and shook their hands, looked in their eyes and asked if they were ready. I told them the eyes were the window to the heart, and I wasn't sure everybody was with us from what I saw.

What had happened to them was a natural matter of human nature. They had received so few positive strokes in football that they had migrated toward the areas where they did get positive strokes—like academics. They didn't want to make an investment in football, because they had all gotten burned.

I should have understood that better but I became very frustrated with them. Really, it was only about 25% who bucked and resisted and were never going to conform. If I had it to do over again, though, I would run off those obvious malcontents because they just drain everybody else.

If that sounds harsh, you have to remember I was coming from Colorado, where we had national championship talent, guys falling all over themselves to beat the other team and guys who had bought into us. I knew it could be that way, and I knew it needed to be that way.

I think my Colorado background was held against me initially. I felt that people thought I was coming from a football factory and were wondering how I'd fit into this situation where football was just something else that happened. I think that outlook was particularly so with academic support.

Somebody had dropped the ball with academic support long before we arrived, and it had a bad hangover effect. We did everything we could to get them to see themselves as being part of the solution. But we clearly weren't all operating with one heartbeat at the time.

Just before that first season, I got reports of players turning up ineligible—players I didn't even know were in academic trouble. This was unfathomable to me, and at Colorado heads would have rolled for allowing this to happen. If I had had the information beforehand, I could have taken disciplinary steps with the players to make sure they were eligible. I would have taken it upon myself to make sure of it.

I expressed my displeasure pretty vigorously. I didn't want to be a bully about it, and I may have come across at times as a bully. But I did want the point made that that type of thing couldn't be tolerated or happen again. It hasn't, and I give academic support great credit for that. We still don't see eye-to-eye on everything, but we sure understand each other better and have come to grips with our differences. I'd say we're compatible, and I'd even say I consider the people over there valuable allies now.

To have so few academic problems on our team, at a school with such rigorous academic demands, is truly amazing. But we had a bad start, and it was two steps forward and one step back for the first few years.

I was having trouble with the training staff then, too. A good trainer is as important as a coach. They have to get kids healed, toughened up and motivated. For instance, I would tell them, "I want a report by 8 A.M. on who's not going to be available to practice today."

They'd say, "Oh, we don't come in that early."

I'd ask, "Well, how are players going to get treatments before classes?"

"We don't come in that early," they would say.

Nobody recognized the significance of training, or they thought the problem was because of me, and it was nearly two years before a change came. Steve Willard arrived from Colorado in 1994, when he was only 29, but he's been perfect as our trainer.

The only place where we found a pleasant surprise was in our strength coach, Larry Lilja. He was Northwestern's football captain in 1974, and one of his brothers later was Michigan's captain and another went on to captain Indiana.

Larry is absolutely the very best. Period. If he marketed himself like some other guys do, he would be the most wanted strength coach in America. He is as valuable a guy as we have in our program. He has terrific insights, which we get a chance to hear when he conducts chapel before games.

A lot of times in the first few months I was guilty of trying to find someone to blame for the things that we couldn't control, probably because there was a galaxy of such things.

Ultimately, we learned to focus on what was in our control. If we were going to teach that, we needed to live it. And early on, how we dealt with the players seemed like all we could influence.

When we began spring practice, though, I got an intimate look at our considerable problems in terms of personnel, too. It wasn't so much our complete lack of speed. It was more that we had no trust between coaches and players. It would have to be painstakingly built.

We had a very talented quarterback, Len Williams, but he was like a wild colt who didn't want to be corraled. He was the best player on the team, he knew it, and he really had been coddled.

Matt O'Dwyer was the best offensive lineman I'd ever been around, but I perceived him to be very selfish. I thought he was out for Matt ... and that was it. I felt I had to tell him that, and it stung him. I think we eventually had a good feeling about each other, but he disliked me for a long time.

We had one key player show up with alcohol on his breath during practice. And when we had our first meetings to teach the systems, the players were just completely lost. The systems were complex, and the players also didn't anticipate the intensity we would demand of them in practice. A lot of them rebelled.

We weren't very good on the field and we had a lot of complications off of it. For all the complaints I had, though, this still was the honeymoon and I actually was kind of giddy. That would soon change.

10.

Grass Stains

*"When nothing seems to help, I go and look at a
stonecutter hammering away at his rock perhaps a
hundred times without as much as a crack showing in it.
Yet at the hundred and first blow it will split in two,
and I know it was not that blow that did it—but
all that had gone before."*
—*Anonymous*

That first year became sort of an expedition to find out how far
behind we were. You know what that year was like? It was like getting rabies shots. I had to get them once, 13 of them in my stomach. But I had to have them.

I kept a diary before and during the 1992 season, and the en-
tries are a good barometer of the growing pains—my own as a
head coach, and the program's. Here they are, with updated
comments:

July 29: *"Daily it seems that no one believes we can do it here.... I keep
on insisting this is a good move."*

As I went around the area to such things as charity golf tour-
naments, I could see that no one believed we would ever win. People seemed to like me, but they felt sorry for the job that I had to
do. All that did was anger me and motivate me.

Another entry I had that day concerned getting cable TV put
in our building. Believe it or not, this was a major, major conces-
sion. There was cable TV all over campus, but nobody wanted to
pay to bring it into the athletic department, like it was some
money pit.

I also wrote about what happened with Dwight Brown, one of
our players. In June Dwight's mother and sister had been mur-
dered by his stepfather in Detroit. Kevin Ramsey was his position
coach, so he went up immediately to see what he could do.

99

Then academic support's Mary Beth Hawkinson—Mother Teresa, Mother Earth—and I were going to go. But Northwestern didn't want to spend the money to send all three of us to Detroit at $120 apiece. We found a way to fly out of O'Hare and back into Midway for less than $100 apiece, so the school agreed to pay. I mean, we were all Dwight had. I think it was always important for Dwight that we went there.

July 30: *"[At the Big Ten media luncheon] I got backed into a corner concerning our team goals. I told them we expected a winning season, and they asked if it was realistic. I hesitated and said, 'Absolutely.' "*
I was introduced that day as Northwestern's 27th head coach. I said, "You know, when you do that math that's one every three-and-a-half years. Try getting a 30-year mortgage with that kind of history." I also said it was nice to see "N.D." on our schedule, and that I was planning to call North Dakota soon to see about exchanging game films.
By the time the grilling was over, I was getting crazy with all the negative things being asked. Another half hour and I might have said, "We'll go to the Rose Bowl this year—I'll show you."

August 4: *"We worked very late and Mary was semi-upset that I had kept the coaches...."*

August 5: *"Realized as I was running today that the key ingredient that is missing at Northwestern is 'ownership'.... No one has any ownership! I must make this happen."*
Ownership was such an elusive commodity here, but I felt it was my responsibility to instill it above and below me. An example of fostering ownership that comes to mind is what we do with our special teams, the grunt work, every year. The coach in charge of each special team—the kickoff return team, the punt team, whatever—makes up invitations for the players he wants on his team. Some of the invitations are extravagant, some are simple, but they back up what I say every year: The best players on our team will be asked to do the special jobs. And if you're not invited, you'd better take a look in the mirror.
"It's only 9:45 and I made all the married guys go home!"

August 6: *"The first real black day ... I found Tim Kish and screamed.... I regained my composure and tried to take everything in stride. But I had already made an ass of myself."*

100

We had learned our best defensive player, Steve Shine, was ineligible, and I went berserk at Tim because he was his position coach. I was really wrong here; I was doing what Mac would have done at Colorado. That was fine for him, but it really wasn't my style and it bothered me later. If I were Catholic, I would have gone to confession. Everything felt like one big train wreck, and the worst was ahead.

"I feel like I'm running out of time. At one time, I felt so organized and the next moment, I feel like I don't have a clue."

August 8: *"I'm so very lucky to have someone who cares so much."*

Mary took me to a restaurant and calmed me down. She just has this sixth sense of when to be that way, and there isn't a person or an animal that she doesn't feel for.

She's an artist and she appreciates the simplest things, as artists often do. And she can get me to do that. She can see the leafless trees against the grey sky and the brown grass and love the beauty of it. Or the shadows that trees or blinds make on a house.

She's also the most unpractical person I've ever known—not a practical bone in her body—while coaches are such creatures of habit and detail. So we work well together—and she loves football. She loves to watch the offensive linemen move because it's like a choreographed dance. We videotape the recruits and their parents when they come in for a visit, and I'll bring the tapes home so Mary can study them, too.

When I accepted the Bear Bryant national coach of the year award after the 1995 season, I said the real reason it was possible was that Mary had taken me where I couldn't take myself. She believed in me when I didn't believe in myself, and together we shared one heartbeat.

August 9: *"Steve Shine got his grade changed, and everyone is happy the teacher had failed to figure in an extra-credit paper. I learned that I need to be patient once more."*

August 15: *"Pat Wright yelled [expletive] as he crossed the finish line [during the 40-yard dash]. Mary was there, and I screamed at him about his language. As he bent over, he threw up on my shoes. What could I say? ... Not a single reporter. No one was interested."*

I was discouraged that in a town of this size, we had no one there from the media. They didn't care.

August 17: *"Practice was very good. I caught myself in the evening*

101

feeling just how I would feel if we were driving for the winning score vs. Notre Dame. I actually felt it. I hope I'm more calm then."

August 18: *"Suddenly tonight, I had this grave reality set in: That we may be really bad. That we probably wouldn't win a game. The possibility exists, and I don't know if I can handle it. But nevertheless, they'll never see me that way.... I made a conscious decision that no matter how bad it was going to be, I was going to be a role model."*

To this day, if you ask our players, I don't think they've ever seen me down. Meanwhile, the number of kids we lost for the season to academic and medical problems was increasing. I was mad at everybody—mad at the administration, mad at the former staff, mad at the trainers, mad at the recruits, mad at myself.

August 19: *"First day of pads ... We can't stop anybody or win a game at this point. It's incredible we are so bad. I'm mad at the former staff."*

When we began our workouts at Northwestern, many of the players were in disbelief at what we expected from them in our workouts. They were nowhere near ready for the physical practices we wanted. I guess we knew that in the spring, though. They hadn't even done live contact drills in the previous few springs.

August 21: *"A beer sounds real good right now, but I'm afraid I've alienated all my coaches and none of them will ask me to go out with them. I'm probably as low as I've been. I was thinking earlier I could have stayed up at C.U., done the bowl games, had a wonderful home, made some money and be in position to get the Missouri job in a year. I may have committed professional suicide. Never to be heard from again!"*

We were up in Kenosha at this time, and I really needed an outlet. But I believed I had angered all my assistants by barking at them so much. I know I never appreciated being yelled at, so I was sure they didn't. I knew I didn't want to behave like that but I just couldn't control myself all the time in the midst of this chaos. I wasn't doing a very good job with crisis management.

August 25: *"At noon today, reality set in (again). I saw the rankings. Colorado was 12th.... I realized just how far down we were. How good the top 50 teams were. How far we have to go. What I left at C.U. And I let myself think that I had genuinely made a mistake. I'm really worried about Courtney and Clay. I had to sit down in the grass after practice as I went back to the dining hall because I had tears from my regrets.*

"I have since regrouped and am pushing forward, but I really need to talk to Mary.... We are probably the worst team in all of Division I. I mean, it is unbelievable how pitiful this group of athletes really is. But they believe in me. Most of them."

After practice, I took the long, scenic way back to the dining room by myself. I like to think on my runs and walks. When I sat in the grass and cried, I was feeling sorry for myself, but I didn't really feel sorry for myself. It's really just the way I motivate myself. It helps me acquire more energy.

It's as though I have to be afraid to really do my best. That was the way it was when I played, and I think I coach the same way. Some people are better the more confident they are. For me, I seem to become more energetic and creative when I'm backed into a corner.

August 30: *"It's almost negligence to put our players on the field with Notre Dame for that period of time. I told our defense to never flinch, that we were going after Notre Dame.... I'm nuts, but I'm thinking that we'll find a way to win. I guess that's why I'm a coach!"*

If those sound like contradictions, you've got to remember how it is that I'm motivated. On the Sunday before every game, there isn't any way we can beat anybody. I don't care who it is. There's no way we can beat them. But by Wednesday, we've found a way to do it. And I'm so cocksure of our plan that I can't wait to see it work.

So in order to understand what I was doing here, you've got to understand me and the way I operate. When I looked at our team and said we were terrible, part of that was so I could reach rock bottom. Because I knew we were going to climb up from there.

September 2: *"I blew up at Phil Burton because he almost broke Pat Wright's ankle. I realized what an impact I could have—negatively, of course."*

September 3: *"We sprung the black jerseys on [the players], and I think they liked them."*

September 5: *"Game day [at Soldier Field] ... I wasn't as nervous as I thought I would be ... it was a beautiful day for a game. The kids looked great in their black jerseys. We came out, and [Lou] Holtz told me what a tough job he had.... We took the opening kickoff and marched to the 17. It was a thing of beauty."*

We lost 42–7 and got outrushed 261–1 in the second half.

But I actually felt okay. Glad it was over. As for the black jerseys, well....

Clay *really* had not wanted to move from Colorado. He was livid about it. He complained about everything, even the way Northwestern's uniforms looked. So to get him involved and thinking positively, I said, "Give me a better idea. How would you do the uniforms?" He said, "Dad, the two hottest colors are purple and black." He drew up the concept of the uniform with these colors, and I had some prototypes made up.

Maybe it runs in the family—I've always loved doing uniforms. Most guys don't like that stuff, but I always got into it. So when we got the uniform the way we wanted it to look, I took it to one administrator who had been here a long time and he said, "Absolutely not."

When I took it to an administrator who hired me, he said, "If you've got the guts to wear them, I'll back you." I actually was apprehensive about the design and figured we'd eventually go back to purple. We kept the black a secret before the season and even had our team picture taken in white jerseys. In fact, we warmed up in purple jerseys before the game.

When we hit the field in black just before the game I think everybody over the age of 40 gasped and almost had heart attacks. But everybody under the age of 40 loved them, and every recruit that's walked in here has, too.

September 6: "*After looking at the films, I was fuming. I didn't get on the defensive coaches because I knew they were all embarrassed.*"

September 7: "*As the day went on, the defense just kept eating at me. Then as we went through kickoff and kickoff return, the kids were all out joking around and I lost it. I told them they didn't care enough to win. Didn't hurt them enough to lose. I swore and felt bad later. It's going to be interesting to see how they respond.*"

I just didn't think they were investing enough of themselves. Lack of ownership was the issue. It was somebody else's problem, and somebody else's fault. I remember losing it, but part of it was by design. I was demanding a standard.

September 12: "*A good run along the Charles River ... and we proceeded to get our asses kicked [by Boston College]. I was thoroughly embarrassed. 35–0 at half. We couldn't tackle or block. It was a disaster. Our coaches couldn't adapt or adjust. It was a total breakdown. I was calm at halftime, but that didn't seem to help. I did not have the pulse of this team.*

"Afterward, I didn't want to see anyone. However, at the half I decided I couldn't be upset. This was an afternoon, an opportunity, I was in Boston with our kids coaching football on a Saturday afternoon. Beautiful day. I might as well make the most of it. Long trip home—but we made it."

I can remember telling the kids after the game, "You know, as bad as this is, there isn't anything in my life I'd rather be doing than be right here coaching you guys."

It was one of those days where we just took our lumps. For us, I think Boston College might have been rock bottom. We had to get there eventually. We had to know where it was.

September 13: *"I got up, read the paper and they took it easy on us. Claiming Boston College was great. In reality, this is the worst football team I've ever seen.... We all knew it was going to be rough, but the Notre Dame game lulled us to sleep, gave us a false sense of where we actually were."*

September 17: *"I have begun to realize just how hard this job is going to be. Talking to Mac convinced me. He said, 'You probably won't win a game.'"*

September 18: *"I'm just hoping we don't embarrass ourselves [against Stanford]. These are good kids. I want so badly to make them into a winning group."*

The last thing I want to do is have any player on the 1992 team think that I thought they were just bad football players, or that they didn't play hard. Because for the most part, they gave me everything they had. And there wasn't a game I didn't think we were going to win.

I think the story, as much as anything that happened here, is that we coached and approached every game as the step that would get us to the top of the hump. I approached each season the same way.

What this approach does is get you to focus and believe and creates an importance to every game and season; if you could focus all your energies on winning that game, on finding a way to win *that* game, it could put you on top of the hump that you needed to get over. I wanted to get to the top of that hump so I could see what the other humps were.

In essence, that's what I think the Northwestern story has been about: the way that we were able to go to that next game and believe that it would be *the* game—and that if we didn't get

105

over the hump, that was okay because we would in the next game.

September 19: "*We fell behind 35–10, then rallied to 35–24 and actually had a chance.... I secretly was relieved and encouraged. I can't let them have a letdown now against Purdue. We have two weeks to prepare, and that should help.*"

September 20: "*Relaxed for the first time.*"

September 22: "*I met with the coaches and told them we could win the Big Ten. Some looked at me like I was nuts.*"

I believed it. Considering the way our coaches could coach and the kinds of improvements I felt we could make, I thought we could win. Sometimes, such belief comes from being too close to it all, whereas if you back away you can see that, boy, there are a lot of steps to go. I chose to get real close.

October 9: "*We decided to do a T-shirt: 'Expect Victory, Purdue '92.' I met with the players ... and challenged them to wear them onto the field against Purdue (in warmups). I told them that 'Expect Victory' was a statement about them, telling the world what it could expect from them....*"

I broke the blackboard at our team meeting that morning (October 3) before we went on the field. I knew I was going to pound it, although I didn't necessarily plan on breaking it. Purdue billed us for it. It was worth it. I was just reaching, trying to get the kids excited. We won 28–14, and I was pleased that our kids were happy but not obnoxious.

October 11: "*We just lost to Indiana. I was a jerk with our offensive coaches. The defense played great but our offense couldn't move. It was a frustrating missed opportunity.... I felt terrible and apologized Sunday to the coaches.*"

October 24: "*Lou Tepper [the Illinois coach] had said, 'You have one guy who's really good.' He meant that O'Dwyer was a great player, but I took his statement out of context and made it appear that [he said] we only had one guy. I made up a handout and showed our kids. I could feel the electricity when they crumpled up the sheets.... Then I gave them a T-shirt saying, 'More Than One,' meaning one Big Ten–quality player.*"

That was a little sneaky, especially since Lou and I are good friends, but I was creating a cause. We fell behind 19–3 at half-time, anyway, but then we had the greatest comeback in Northwestern history and won 27–26 with 13 seconds left. Our quarterback, Len Williams, was perfect, and our receivers, Chris Gamble and Lee Gissendaner, were incredible. As you watched the game unfold, you knew what was going to happen. It was like a tidal wave.

To me, the Illinois game was a watershed. The win would now be a part of our program, and we have pictures from "The Comeback" framed in the entrance to our building.

November 1: *"The official said it [the last-second field goal] was wide, and we lost 27–26 [to Michigan State]. The replay on one of the student's cameras showed that we made it, but there was nothing we could do."*

You have to just let go of games like this. You lost. Period. We had had a chance to go ahead earlier but couldn't convert a two-point conversion. And we turned the ball over four times. Yes, we had a chance to win it at the end on a 35-yard field goal, and maybe the official was wrong. But we had other opportunities that officials had nothing to do with, and those are the things that you've got to take care of yourself.

You can't turn the game over to the other team to see if they're going to win it or lose it, and you can't turn it over to the officials to see if they're going to win it or lose it. You've got to take care of things yourself. That's what I mean by accountability.

November 8: *"I probably tugged on Superman's cape this week. [Ron Vanderlinden] and the defensive coaches complained about Michigan's no-huddle substitutions, and I made a point of it in my press conference. It became national news.... As if, 'Even if Michigan was using the rules to its advantage, why would Northwestern University bother to complain?' Michigan just reinforced my bitter opinion of this program. They were jerks, except for Les Miles.... After the game, [a 40–7 loss, Michigan coach Gary] Moeller wouldn't shake my hand, and neither did any of the other Michigan coaches except Miles."*

I gave up on the diary at this point, but there were significant developments during the last two weeks of the season. We were 2–7 at the time, and now we faced Iowa.

We put Iowa in red letters on our schedule because we wanted to create a rivalry—like Mac had done by red-lettering Nebraska. I wanted to red-letter Michigan, but we didn't have Michigan on the schedule in two of the five years I had a contract for. Nor could I red-letter Ohio State, because we didn't play the Buckeyes two of those years.

When I was at Colorado the team that I hated to recruit against in the Midwest was Iowa because they did such a good job. For years, I really, really envied what they had done. I thought highly of their coach, Hayden Fry. So as I looked for a program to emulate, I decided it would be Iowa. Iowa had about destroyed Northwestern every year since 1973. When we beat Iowa, we could say we had arrived.

But it was difficult to get the rivalry stoked in 1992. It didn't help our cause that we had seven or eight kids late for a team meeting that week, and I went ballistic on them. They were all kids that I'd had some trouble with before, and I kept them out of the game.

So we had a bad taste in our mouths as a team when we went to Iowa. And we got embarrassed. Absolutely embarrassed— 56–14. They even kicked an onside kick to rub it in.

After the game, Coach Fry came over and said, "Hope we didn't hurt any of your boys." I sort of stared at him and said, "I don't think so." His comment stuck with me for four years.

Wisconsin was our last game, and the Badgers were 5–5 and had a bowl game wrapped up if they could beat us—which by all indications they should have done. But they turned the ball over a couple of times, and lo and behold, we were ahead late in the game. They were driving but Greg Gill came in on a blitz for us and caused a fumble and we won 27–25.

This was our first home win, and the fans tried to tear down the goalposts after the game ... only to discover that we had them encased in concrete and greased up. I had asked in the school paper that our student body not do that because it was an insult. I even went out and tried to pull kids off the goalposts. They didn't really respond to me, but they couldn't get the goalposts down, either.

It was our third Big Ten win—the first time in 20 years such a thing had happened at Northwestern. And Lee Gissendaner, who led the country in punt returning, returned a kickoff for a touchdown, and had 68 receptions, received the Silver Football award from the *Chicago Tribune* as the best player in the Big Ten.

No Northwestern player had won the Silver Football award

since 1970. People were stunned. But it really gave us credibility for recruiting. I thought we were way ahead of schedule. I mean, I had been fully prepared for the possibility of going 0–11.

11.

Fool's Gold

"Trust is the emotional glue that binds followers and leaders together. The accumulation of trust is a measure of the legitimacy of leadership...."
—*Dennis Kroner*

I wasn't as upbeat after the 1993 season. We started 2–1, then we lost. And lost. And lost.

After the sixth straight, somebody asked what it felt like. I said it was as if I had a pencil stuck in my eye, and every time we lost it was like somebody was jamming that pencil a half-inch deeper in my eye.

After the last game of the season, when we had lost eight in a row, I told Mary, "I'm pulling this pencil out of my eye." It was such a relief.

At the beginning of the '93 season it seemed like we had a lot of reasons to feel good about our prospects. I had told our quarterback, Len Williams, that I didn't want him back unless it was on my terms, and he had a conversation with his mother about it. She told him, "Do you have any idea what this group of coaches has done for you? Do you realize how much is at your fingertips?" From that point on, Len was just a different guy. He was still cocky, but that's okay in a quarterback.

Then we had been able to recruit a talented class—ranked among the top 25 by one service and in about the top 35 by another. Of course, most of the kids weren't going to be ready to play for two or three years, but that high a ranking was unheard of for Northwestern.

One thing the recruiting gurus can't measure, however, is "fit," and I neglected to consider that in at least one case—and was emphatically reminded of why it matters so much.

We went after a highly recruited player, Eric Scott, from the Los Angeles area, even though our kids didn't feel right about him after his visit here. I dismissed their reservations and ended up going well beyond my own rules of treating people consistently with him. I gave him more leeway than anybody—special privileges, almost—and created a bad situation.

Eric had come from an awful neighborhood, one where we had to visit him during the day because it was too rough at night. I think that's part of why I wanted him to fit in here. I thought about how much Northwestern could do for him and his family. I think I also was being a little greedy. I really hope that I wanted him more for himself than for us but I'm not sure I can say I did.

Eric came but the whole time he was here he was grumpy. Everybody tried to please him but nothing could make him happy. He did some good things but his presence disrupted attitude and chemistry. He left after the first season but left behind a lesson.

The end of the recruiting period always is a scramble, like trying to solve a Rubik's Cube, and this year's was a perfect example. By the end we had more players who wanted to come than we had scholarships for. We had two scholarships left and about four guys out there, a couple of whom still hadn't decided where they wanted to go.

Pat Fitzgerald and Hudhaifa Ismaeli were two of the guys in this batch. We had called them as signing day closed in and said we had to have answers. Well, it got to be 1:30 that day and we had no answers. I had a flight to Louisville to visit a fullback who was also in the mix. Meanwhile, I had John Wristen staked out in Colorado to go see another player if none of these guys worked out.

When I got off the plane I immediately called the office. Still no answers. Fitz, I was told, was in a conference with his dad and his high school coach, and we couldn't reach Hudhaifa. So I picked up my rental car and called from the car phone. By now Hudhaifa had committed and we had one scholarship left. Fitz still was in conference, so I drove to the fullback's house in Louisville. I was supposed to be at his house at six.

At five minutes of six I pulled up two houses away and called the office: Fitz had committed. So I had Rob Chiavetta call this kid two doors down from me to tell him I couldn't make it. Fitz and Hudhaifa became very significant in our program, but it was so close to not working out.

Every year it's that way. It never works out the way you think it's going to or for the reasons you've figured it will. You do all this evaluating and research and selling ... and you still can't ever be sure how it will go or why.

I remember sitting in his house with Tim Scharf, one of our linebackers, and he said, "I'm coming to Northwestern to show all the other big schools that I can play." That wasn't quite the same as saying, "I love Northwestern, and I really want to play for you," but it still worked for me.

We introduced Steve Musseau at Camp Kenosha that year, and his plan was to work on trust. This was the primary illustration he gave us:

"There was a world-famous tightrope walker, who had reached the age where he wanted to retire. But before he retired he wanted to do something spectacular, something no one else had ever done. So he decided he was going to stretch a tightrope across Niagara Falls and walk across that rope.

"As you know, at Niagara Falls the wind blows quite hard, and if the spray from the falls got on the rope it could become very slick. They advertised his walk in the newspapers, on television, and on the radio. The moment of truth came, and there were thousands of people who came to see him.

"No one had ever done this before, and as the tightrope walker steps onto the platform and balances himself on the rope, the whole crowd starts to cheer, yell and scream. He gets about halfway across, carrying his long, long pole in his hands, when he slips and almost falls. The crowd is petrified. They think he is going to fall but he regains his balance and makes it across. The crowd erupts. They have never seen anything like it.

"He had done the impossible, and now he turns around to go back. The crowd screams, 'Oh, no, he's not going back again.' Sure enough, he picks up his pole and starts back. About three-quarters of the way, he again slips and almost falls. The crowd is again somewhat petrified, but he regains his balance and they clap, but not as much. After all, he had done it once before.

"Now he gets a wheelbarrow, and the crowd says, 'Oh, no, surely he's not going to try to push that wheelbarrow across.' About a quarter of the way over he slips but regains his balance, and boy, oh boy, the crowd erupts again. Wow! He'd done something no one else had ever done.

"So he turns around and puts the wheelbarrow back on the rope and the crowd yells, 'You're not going to do that again, are you?' And he says, 'Do you believe that I could put somebody in the wheelbarrow and roll it across?' The crowd says, 'We believe, we believe.' And he points to this one guy and says, 'Alright—you first!'

"This is the difference between belief and trust. It's easy to believe, but the trust to sit in that wheelbarrow is quite a different thing. When you are participating in any competitive event, you have to be willing to sit in the wheelbarrow. If you don't, you don't trust. You've got to trust your neighbor, you've got to trust your coaches, you've got to trust the guy laying himself out next to you.

"Who's going to sit in the wheelbarrow?"

During the practice sessions at Kenosha I believed the team came to understand Steve's message and had reached a certain level of unity, and I was eager to start the 1993 season.

But when we opened against Notre Dame the first play from scrimmage should have been a hint of what was to come that fall. We ran a bootleg pass that bounced off Luther Morris' helmet and was returned for a touchdown. At halftime, however, we were only losing 10–6, and the television reporter asked me what I was going to tell my team. I said, "I'm going to ask my players to get in the wheelbarrow." Of course he had no idea what I was talking about.

Notre Dame fumbled to open the second half and we scored to go ahead 12–10. A lovely hush descended over Notre Dame Stadium. But Notre Dame went right down the field on the next series, and ultimately our defense couldn't hold up. We lost 27–12.

I thought we lost because we didn't know how to win, didn't know how to seize the game. This is what happens in programs that haven't won. It's part of an evolutionary process. I told the kids the table had been set, but we didn't eat the dinner.

The press tried to make this into a moral victory, but I refused. I was angry—well, discouraged—that we hadn't taken advantage of the opportunity Notre Dame had given us and we had set up.

Next, again, was Boston College. The Eagles had embarrassed us the year before. This season, B.C. had lost a close opener to Miami, and a *Boston Herald* sportswriter wrote an article noting that there was "plenty of plankton" left on the schedule. If they couldn't get the big fish, well, they still had us.

I put the plankton comment on the overhead projector for our players. I don't know what it did for them, but it worked wonders for me.

We won 22–21, which was a tremendous upset and a tremendous moment for our program. Boston College was a good football team. When I went over to shake coach Tom Coughlin's hand, I could see he was devastated. I would have been, too.

That game earned us some votes in the polls, and now we had a sense of strength and a game with Wake Forest. I had worked with their new coach, Jim Caldwell, at Colorado, and I knew he was in a tough spot. For the first time at Northwestern, I went into a game knowing we had an advantage on both sides of the ball.

The game was played in an absolute downpour and our field didn't drain much, so water was just standing on it. But we won 26–14, and now, for the first time in about two decades, Northwestern was ranked. We were turning the corner.

It was fool's gold.

Our players' mentality now was that winning was something you could just turn on and off, and I couldn't get across to them that there was a fallacy in that thinking.

By the time we played Ohio State a week later we had a number of offensive linemen hurt. We didn't even have enough bodies to use real offensive linemen for our scout team, and we had to play some guys against the Buckeyes who weren't even close to ready. We didn't practice very well that week, in addition, and we got crushed 51–3. I thought we'd play better than we did but I wasn't so upset because of our injury situation. I was kidding myself.

We faced Wisconsin the next week, and on the bus ride up to Madison I read Pat Riley's book, *The Winner Within*. I was engrossed, and it stimulated me to stay up late that night thinking of what I wanted to tell the team. By the time I met with them on game morning, I felt like a preacher. I was so convinced that what I was going to say was going to make a difference.

I had never been so emotional with my team, but I may have been too emotional. I made our players uptight, and then Wisconsin was really jacked up to play us since we knocked them out of the bowl scene in 1992. It was an awful combination.

They ran over us like we weren't even there and beat us to a pulp 53–14. They didn't run that score up on us, either. If you don't make a team punt all day, you can't blame anybody but yourself.

Two games in a row, we'd allowed more than 50 points. I was so upset, so embarrassed that in the days after the game I compounded the situation—at least for the time being. What I did was a massive mistake, for that minute, anyway, and it probably fractured or maybe even destroyed the rest of the season.

115

I decided I should call a meeting of all the kids I had inherited. I deliberately left out the kids we had recruited. I was sure separating them was the right thing to do. Part of the reason was that most of the kids we'd recruited weren't playing much yet, but the main point was that I didn't think the older guys were committed.

"I didn't recruit you guys," I began, "so you may not trust me or be as committed to winning as the guys whose homes I sat in and recruited. But we're all in this together."

My words and tone became increasingly animated and everything I wanted to convey came out with the opposite meaning of what I'd consciously intended. I divided our team emotionally. Those guys felt like I didn't want them and that I only cared about the guys we had recruited.

The message I had wanted to send was, "Hey, you guys are the ones playing, and you need to be accountable to each other." I used the wrong words, though, and because of me the squad was in disarray. As soon as the meeting broke up there were all kinds of harsh words in the locker room, and the younger kids received the brunt of them.

My coaches didn't think I had done the right thing and wanted me to call another meeting to try to pull everybody back together and get it all resolved. I didn't want to do it and I didn't want to hear them. Today, I would say I made a mistake. Then, I was dead-set that I was right.

I wasn't right, although I do think the meeting eventually helped: I believe it actually inspired a great deal of trust from the players that we had recruited—and left out of the meeting—and helped develop a bond among them.

It may be a rationalization but I think 1995 partly was an extension of that bond.

After that, well, we plunged.

We lost to Minnesota the next week 28–26 on one of the flukiest endings I've ever seen. We got a first down in field-goal range on a Gissendaner catch with about three seconds left. But the clock operator—this is at Dyche Stadium, now—let it run down to one second before stopping it. Still, we had a chance to try a field goal. Or so we thought.

As our field-goal team went out, the official standing over center said, "You can't snap this until I tell you." As he's standing there, the head referee blew the whistle to start the clock. The official standing over the center didn't back out of the way until the

116

whistle blew so by the time our kid put his hands on the ball time had expired! We snapped it back and the ball was kicked through but, of course, it didn't count.

It's one thing for something like that to happen on the road but it's not supposed to happen at home. Clearly, our own people cost us our last chance. I was mad at everybody, mad at our whole place. I was told they'd fire the guy in charge of the clock but that never happened.

In the end I know it wasn't because of him we lost the game. But it was really hard not to look for somebody to be the scapegoat.

Since then, every day in practice I create a situation with one second left on the clock and we kick without a snap count. Now we have a standard game rule: If fewer than five seconds remain, we snap the ball on the referee's whistle. If a situation like that ever happens again we're going to be the only team in the country prepared for it.

After the Minnesota game we collapsed and never got back into the season. As it was, morale was down from the meeting and after the players put so much into that game they just wouldn't reinvest themselves again.

Indiana beat us 24–0 and the only thing memorable about it was the officials penalizing Pat Wright for blocking below the waist. Well, Pat was only 5'3", and I told the official, "Where's he supposed to block him?" I called Pat over and said, "Now look at him: Is he supposed to jump to be able to hit the guy above the waist?" The official could only laugh, but we still got the penalty.

After a 20–13 loss to Illinios, we had an ugly episode with Michigan State. A brawl broke out and one of our players hit one of theirs over the head with a wooden chair. I always felt Michigan State pushed the envelope of clean play but I wasn't going to stand for our players getting into stuff like that.

We lost the game 31–29 and probably lost the fight. I suspended one player for two games and five others for the next game against Iowa. I also had a player call the Michigan State coach, George Perles, to apologize. Later that week, Iowa week, I threw a player out of a team meeting for screwing around and didn't dress him for the game. That was too bad because his parents came to watch. He ended up quitting.

Iowa beat us 23–19, then we lost our eighth in a row to Penn State 43–21. Reporters from Penn State asked how I felt about the attendance, which was about 24,000, and how I could stand this situation having come from Colorado. I didn't have a real answer. I just said we'd have to put a better product on the field before we could expect attendance to improve.

Really, we were low. Yet as miserably as that season unfolded, especially after the early-season promise, I learned so much. All that happened was essential to our metamorphosis—and my own growth.

For instance, I had allowed myself to get distracted about a month into the season. Kellen Winslow, the former Missouri and San Diego Chargers star tight end, called me when we were 2–1 and wanted to discuss the possibility of the Missouri job. It looked like Bob Stull and his staff were going to be out, and Kellen, who at the time was broadcasting M.U. games, was being considered for the athletic director's job.

How could I not be interested in Missouri? It had been my dream to be the head coach there. I listened to Kellen, and I started getting vibes from people around the state that it was something I might legitimately have a shot at. A kind of grass-roots movement got started for me, a letter-writing campaign.

But Dan Devine was running the search and I just don't think he considered me. Whatever the reason, I didn't get an interview. Then we lost eight in a row and whatever chance I had was gone. It all probably served me right for taking my eye off the stepping stones and looking at the stream.

12.

Keno-where

"Strength is the product of struggles."
—G.J. Cielec

Kenosha is a coach's dream. When we first walked out to the practice field there, in fact, I called it the Field of Dreams.

Players might perceive it less pleasantly. The first year Steve Musseau was there, 1993, he asked them how they spelled pain. They didn't know what he meant, so he spelled it out: K-E-N-O-S-H-A. When we left there in 1992 I handed out camouflage T-shirts that said "Camp Kenosha" on them.

Originally, I was concerned that it was a little cushier there than it should be. But we make up for the air conditioned rooms with features like the locker room, which is actually a wrestling room. We try to ventilate it the best we can but it doesn't smell great.

What I like best about Kenosha is that it's so isolated. There's nothing there when we're there. "Keno-where," one of the kids called it when we were headed there on the bus the first year. I told the kids that one of the reasons we were going was because there wasn't any way home. It's like the Hotel California: Once you checked in, you had to stay.

The day we leave Kenosha is total jubilation for the players. But right now if I told our seniors we weren't going back, they wouldn't accept it. You've got to go through Kenosha and I think our players will tell you that it is one of the reasons we became a Rose Bowl team and the Big Ten champs.

We don't take our team pictures until after Kenosha, because I don't want anybody who didn't survive Kenosha in that picture. And the reason I don't conduct our elections for captains until that time is I want to see who stands out in the face of all this adversity and comes to the forefront and leads. I want the players to see who steps up at the really tough times.

Kenosha is a time in which there's only one focus, and it's a time that represents real mental toughness. It means getting ready. We go from six in the morning until lights out at 10:45; some of the guys, though, don't go to sleep until midnight or later because it's their chance to blow off steam.

That's okay, too. It's intended to be a total bonding experience. From the time you get there you can feel everyone growing together.

It takes the freshmen a little longer to get acclimated, though. They feel sorry for themselves, because, really, they are clueless. They get what our kids call "Kenosha-face." It's this blank stare out into space that says, "What am I doing here? I didn't know it was going to be like this." When you see that, that's when you know it's time to connect the kid with one of the older guys who's had Kenosha-face himself.

Two years ago, Chris Leeder, a freshman offensive lineman, got Kenosha-face. During practice one morning I looked around and Chris wasn't there. When I asked where he was one of the other freshmen said, "Well, Coach, he may have left."

I said, "Left?! How did he leave? There's no way for him to leave."

"We think he called a cab," the freshman replied.

Sure enough, Chris had called a cab and snuck down through the trees behind the parking lot to catch it. He took it to Chicago, a $150 ride. Then he got on a train and headed back to his home in Michigan.

We called his parents that afternoon and his dad said, "I'll take care of this." He picked up Chris at the station, and I called him that night and challenged him a little bit. His family put him in the car and drove him back to Kenosha the next day.

If you leave, obviously, you've bailed out on the other guys. And part of what you're saying is, "I'm not tough enough to take this." So the kids can be pretty cruel. As they call it, it's Social Darwinism (remember, we're at Northwestern). If you're not tough enough to take Kenosha, well, then you're not tough enough to play with them.

So I had to sit down with the players and beg them to try to understand that Chris was a freshman and that he was just overwhelmed. I said, "You don't have to just let him walk in here like nothing happened, but you've got to give him a chance."

After about a week Chris was fine. Now it's something we all laugh about. Last year when I brought the freshmen in I had Chris stand up, and I asked if he still remembered the cab number and what it cost to go to Chicago. "If anybody wants a ride out," I told them, "Chris will make the arrangements for you." So it's funny now. Part of Kenosha lore.

Coach Vince Okruch once took KeJaun DuBose, a defensive tackle, up to talk to Vince's son's grade school class. To get there, they took the road that heads in the direction of Kenosha. Ke-Jaun said, "Coach Okruch, isn't this, isn't this ... the same direction as Kenosha?" Vince had to calm KeJaun down.

Making the initial arrangements for us to go to Kenosha in our budget-oriented climate was a bit of an ordeal, but it wasn't as difficult as you might think. In actual per-person expenses, it's cheaper for us to go to Kenosha than it is to stay on campus. Northwestern charges us more for room and board than Kenosha does.

Extra expenses came from our weight room, laundry, the buses and paying for use of the facilities up there. Much of those expenses now are covered by boosters so it's hard to argue against going, especially with the return we get, or at least the return we feel like we get.

I don't know if everybody in our athletic department understands this, but the truth is we always are conscious of being prudent about expenses. I don't think there's any reason to be abusive in spending, anyway. If we can save a buck, we save a buck.

A lighter side to the bonding in Kenosha is our rookie show. The show really helps the freshmen come together and gives them a chance to throw back some of the stuff that the veterans and coaches have been throwing at them for three weeks. It takes nerve and guts to do some of the acts they come up with.

The second year we were in Kenosha, we had just finished doing six TV commercials for the season, and the freshmen put together a video spoof on some of those ads. Hudhaifa Ismaeli could do Buckwheat from the *Little Rascals* perfectly, and at the end of each clip Hudhaifa was somewhere saying, "O-tay!" Northwestern was refurbishing our library at the time and didn't have walls up between the stalls in the bathroom, so the guys did a satire about getting closer as a team—with six guys sitting on the seats passing toilet paper up and down. The video was one of the funniest things I've ever seen.

Basically, though, all day, it's football. Three practices, meetings, etc. Every night at nine is my hour. It's when I get to teach the kids, which I treasure because I don't get to connect with them personally much in practice.

121

When I was a position coach, I loved the teaching part, trying to get the players to see and know what I knew. I need to be able to look at them and tell them what I see and feel, and I don't always get to do that on the field any more.

My topics vary. It was during this time, for instance, that last year I'd get the scale out and put a penny on it, or not put a penny on it, before I dismissed them. I'll talk about character one night, dealing with agents another night. We'll talk about redshirting. We'll talk about gambling. We'll talk about date rape. I try to address everything that needs to be said. It's like having an hour with your son and trying to get him ready for life.

It's also during this 9:00 hour that Steve Musseau spends 15-20 minutes with the team. His first year, of course, he had focused on the meaning and value of trust. In 1994 his message was patience, and his main story revolved around a hunting trip he had taken with two assistant coaches when he was in Idaho.

"It was about 105 degrees, and we forgot to bring water and so were practically dying of thirst. We decided to go to a farmhouse to get water. But none of the farmhouses had anybody in them. Finally, we went to this one house that in the back had an old handle they used to pump water out of the ground. I had been used to those when I was growing up, and I thought maybe we could make it work.

"Since Herb was the youngest, John and I told Herb he should be the one to pump. He started pumping and pumping, and it was hot and he was sweating and he said, 'Coach, I don't believe there's any water down there.'

" 'Oh my gosh,' I said, 'we forgot to prime the pump. You've got to put some water in there to get it started.' We looked down the hill, and there was a stream. It wasn't very clean, but we got a rusty tin can and filled it up with water and poured it down the pump.

"Still, Herb was pumping and sweating, pumping and sweating. He said, 'Coach, I don't think there's any water in there,' and he quits pumping. I said, 'Don't quit now! If you stop pumping, the water will go all the way back down and these wells are about 200 feet deep.'

"Herb starts pumping again, and he's sweating and breathing hard and can hardly do it any longer when, finally, he gets a trickle of water out of the pump. And as he pushed the handle up and down it begins to gush out. Once he got it flowing, he barely had to move the handle.

"It's the same way with the Northwestern football team. You've got to prime the pump, and the water is real deep down there and you can't

*quit. If you quit it goes all the way back down to the bottom and you
have to start all over again.*

*"Once you get pumping you've got to just keep on pumping and pretty
soon you will find a little water coming out of there. When it starts to flow,
you'll notice you won't have to move the handle very hard to have a great,
big stream of water. You can't quit because the water might be just six
inches away. Six inches away, and you get enough water to last you a
lifetime."*

We used "priming the pump" as our motto for that year, and we
took an old pump with us to every game. In fact, we actually stuck
it up outside one of the practice fields at Kenosha and all the kids
would hit the pump once as they came off the field.

Another thought I tried to get across was the dramatic difference between being about "WE" instead of about "ME." I put a
big "M" and a big "E" on the overhead for our first team meeting
that season and said that the only thing we had to turn around
was that "M."

Then I turned it upside down on the overhead and said, "The
whole secret comes down to this one simple word that, if it's read
the right way, will make the right things happen for us."

As badly as we had collapsed at the end of 1993 we entered
1994 brimming with hope. Not that anybody else thought we
should be.

On August 22, *Sports Illustrated* did a "Too Good to Be True"
feature, which included a fake cover saying, "8–0 Northwestern
Locks Up Rose Bowl Bid." I guess the idea was that it was something outside of the realm of possibility.

Somebody this season had that picture blown up and wrote,
"Oh Ye of Little Faith" on it.

We'd had another recruiting class I liked, and I was happy
about how we'd refined our on-field system. Wisconsin had
gone on to win the Rose Bowl the previous season, and I had
been impressed with what the Badgers had done with the running game. Among our problems was that we could not run the
football and couldn't stop the run on defense. I know there's a
correlation, so we changed our emphasis to become more run-
oriented.

Still, we needed consistency at quarterback after losing Len
Williams, and we never got comfortable there in 1994. That cast,
specifically Steve Schnur, gelled in 1995, but we could never find
the right rhythm or combination in '94.

Our difficulties led to some thorny times with our student paper. They had a writer who was absolutely abusive and he began referring to Schnur and Tim Hughes as "Beavis and Butthead." He also compared Hudhaifa Ismaeli's name to a contagious disease. I couldn't understand where his mean spirit was coming from so I invited him out to dinner. I told him, "I don't get it. I'm paid to do my job so you have the right to rip me. But where do you get off ripping Hudhaifa and Steve Schnur and Tim Hughes so personally?"

He said, "Well, they get scholarships. They're paid."

What came across was a deep resentment toward athletes who get scholarships, especially if they don't perform up to expected levels. He said, "You see my role as a cheerleader," but I told him I didn't see it that way at all. I've always opened myself up and talked about everything with the media. I'm very approachable and I realize that fair criticism is to be expected.

I wanted to make peace or at least have him understand my point. But he was a real smart-ass and by the time we finished the meal, I wanted to smash his face into the lasagna I was buying him. I held back. When we walked out he didn't have enough money to tip the valet guy so I tipped the valet for him.

After that I said, "That's it." We took a no-talk stand with the student newspaper for the rest of that season. I guess they got us back by writing in the spring of '95 that I was one of the reasons Northwestern would never win.

I really try to be objective in understanding what the press writes. I don't know that I always achieve that, but I do my best to see where they come from. To me, though, this student reporter was clearly unfair and abusive.

We lost the 1994 opener to Notre Dame 42–15 when their freshman quarterback Ron Powlus threw three touchdown passes in the first quarter. That was rough because our secondary was the last place I had concerns.

Then we tied Stanford 41–41. I wanted that win particularly badly because their coach, Bill Walsh, had been critical of me when he was a broadcaster during one of the Orange Bowls and had made some disparaging remarks about Northwestern in Lowell Cohn's book *Rough Magic*. I once wrote in my diary, *I want to beat Walsh in the worst way.*

At least the tie was enough to upset Coach Walsh; he did not come over to shake my hand after the game. I followed him down to the locker room, but I finally gave up about the 10-yard-line.

124

He did later come into our locker room but he wouldn't do it out in front of the stands.

Before the next game, against Air Force, I sensed we were at a pivotal point of the season and tried a few different approaches to reaching and unifying the team.

At a team meeting that week I said, "You know, who are we? What are we about here? We need a word to describe us as a football team, what we want to be as a football team." So we went around the room and the word we came up with was "relentless."

I asked players to come up with names of players they thought were relentless, and whether they thought they had ever played relentlessly. They came up with Boston College the year before. I asked every one of them to give me a sort of picture with words of what relentlessness meant to them.

We decided we would now use the word relentless as the standard for every block, every tackle, every assignment. This gave me license to ask, "Is that a relentless block?" It struck a nerve with the players. "Relentlessness" became the criterion for Northwestern football, and that's what the players became accountable to produce.

I had another idea that was inspired by a Steve Musseau story. He had told me about a coach who'd had T-shirts made up with a mysterious acronym on them. When a reporter asked one of the players what it meant, the player said, "I can't tell you. And if I told you, I'd have to kill you."

When we came up with the word "relentless," for some reason I thought back to that story. I came up with a T-shirt with the acronym "A.R.T." on it. Before I handed the shirts out, I met with our coaches and said the only people who can know what this stands for are our players and the ten coaches in this room. Nobody else: secretaries, trainers, equipment managers, nobody. Even your wives can't know. It's so serious that if your wife knows, I've got to kill her or you've got to kill her.

Now, that sounded pretty gruesome, but I thought it was a way to promote more closeness among us.

Of course, the players laughed out loud when I told them what our agreement would be. But they wore the T-shirts around our hotel in Colorado Springs the night before the game and a couple of people who came to a reception I was having saw some of them around. They told me they'd asked the players what their T-shirts stood for, and the players said they couldn't tell them— and that if they did tell them they'd have to kill them. The people couldn't believe it. I smiled and said, "Well, that's right."

We won the game 14–10 and it was a huge win for us. On the road, at altitude. We were 1-1-1, with Ohio State coming up in two weeks—and I was thinking bowl game.

Our preparation for Ohio State was terrific and we were ahead 9–0 at halftime. At that crucial point, though, our guys were thinking, "Gosh, we're leading Ohio State at halftime," instead of "Let's put these guys away." We kind of putzed around early in the half, and they ended up going ahead 17–9.

We scored a touchdown with about five minutes left in the game and I decided to go for two but it failed. We got the ball back again, but couldn't score, and lost 17–15.

We had played so hard, however, that I was heartened because I felt like we were on the verge of a dramatic breakthrough. After the game, Ohio State's talented running back, Eddie George, said: "Those guys came out with a lot more emotion. I give a lot of credit to Northwestern. They're a good ballclub. They are a force to be reckoned with in the Big Ten."

So I expected a lot out of our next game, against Wisconsin. Again, we led at halftime, 14–10. This time, though, we had an utter collapse. The second half was an absolute clinic by Wisconsin. The Badgers mauled us. It began when the Wisconsin crowd—yes, in our stadium—kept us from hearing our own snap count on a punt near our own end zone. The Badgers were like sharks to blood after that.

The final was 46–14 and that was excruciating for me. I stayed up all night. I couldn't sleep in our bed and I ended up in almost a fetal position on the couch because my gut ached so much. I just couldn't believe that at this stage of our program we couldn't make the necessary adjustments to physically slow them down. I thought we had evolved to a point where that couldn't happen.

I scraped myself up the next morning, with some help from Mary, but I was wondering how I would be able to get the team to keep hitting the pump. The staff was really down, too.

Once I had some objective thoughts about the situation, though, I told the staff, "If what we say to the kids is to have any meaning, we have to conduct ourselves the way we would want them to conduct themselves." We couldn't allow ourselves to mope about the loss.

Larry Lilja told me a story once that had stuck with me, and it popped into my mind during a run later that week. I told the team this story with Larry sitting near me in the front of the room:

"There was a high school team that practiced near a small lake.

126

Across the lake lived Coach Jones, the winningest coach in the history of the state, and he was retired.

"Every day this high school team would come out and practice and practice hard, as hard as they could practice. But no matter how hard they practiced, they couldn't win. Every day, the retired coach would sit in his lawnchair and watch them.

"One day the quarterback of the team decided he was going to go talk to Coach Jones and ask him what he sees, why they can't win. So the quarterback went around the lake and said, 'Coach, I know you watch us practice every day. I know you know how hard we practice. I know you know how to win. Is there anything that you can tell us that can help us win?'

"Coach Jones put his arm around the player and walked him near the edge of the lake. Suddenly, he grabbed the quarterback, thrust his head into the water, and held him down under the water...."

(I abruptly demonstrated this by grabbing Larry and throwing his head back. Even with no water, it grabbed the players' attention.)

"So the kid is about to drown, and Coach Jones pulls him up and says, 'When you want to win as much as you wanted that next breath, then that's when you'll win.'"

That story told what I wanted to tell, and darned if we didn't go out and beat Minnesota 37–31.

Indiana was up next. We had scored a total of nine points against the Hoosiers over the last four seasons. We told the players it was going to be a headache kind of game and handed out Advil when we gave them the scouting report. At the top of the report it said, "Give as needed to appropriate Hoosier."

In chapel before the game Larry showed a video about hyenas and lions. The hyena is the animal that most pesters a lion. It's the only animal that drives a lion nuts because the lion can't catch a hyena and the hyena knows it.

But in the video a lion discovers that a pack of hyenas had gone into its den and taken one of its cubs. The lion chased the hyena and made an incredible leap—beyond what a lion should be able to do. With a single claw, it caught the hyena.

Larry's point was that this was something the lion wanted more than anything so he did more than he should have been able to do. When I talked to the team before the game I showed that video and talked about that story. We won 20–7 and afterwards I asked the players how the hyena tasted.

We were 3-3-1, and we were at the crossroads of getting to a bowl game, with Illinois, Michigan State, Iowa, and Penn State in front of us. Three of those teams were not much better than us. One was significantly better. We had a great opportunity.

But Illinois beat us 28–7 after we were down just 14–7 at half-time, and then Michigan State muscled us all over the field 35–17. It seemed like we would just wear down, physically and emotionally. Then it was Iowa, and we simply did not have the team prepared and lost 49–13. It was probably our most poorly prepared and poorly coached game at Northwestern, and I can't really say why it happened that way.

After Dennis Lundy fumbled in the Iowa game, a rumor reached me that he had been gambling and owed a lot of money. I immediately called Dennis into my office. I fully expected him to deny it. Instead, Dennis said, "Well, I have been gambling, but I didn't fumble the ball on purpose."

I couldn't believe it. I said, "Dennis, do you realize how serious this is? Do you realize this could involve the FBI?" I asked him how he got involved, how much he had been doing. He said he basically had gotten involved to try to make some money to bring his mother up from Florida for a game.

I talked to our athletic director, who was now Rick Taylor, and the next day we arranged to have our legal counsel talk to Dennis and another player who also was involved. On Thursday night, the university called and told me I had to suspend Dennis. I called Dennis and advised him not to say anything to anybody.

When I met with the team the next day, I said Dennis had been suspended for committing a violation and would have to suffer the consequences. One of them was that he would lose his chance to break the Northwestern single-season rushing record held by Bob Christian.

We got beat up 45–17 at Penn State. In place of Dennis, Darnell Autry made his first start and rushed for 171 yards, the most ever by a Northwestern freshman. I was walking off the field with Darnell and Penn State fans were yelling, "Hey, 24, you're too good to go to school there. Why don't you transfer?"

Meanwhile, the media was going crazy trying to find out what had happened with Dennis. I was trying to protect him as much as I could. The news later got out because the university made an announcement about a basketball player involved in gambling and intimated a football player had been suspended for the same offense.

I often wonder what would have become of the situation if it hadn't gotten to me. How far would it have proceeded? Who else might have gotten involved? Would it have just ended of its own accord? I've also wondered whether I had to act. Maybe it would have just blown over and no damage would have been done.

But I always tell my players and staff that when they're in a quandary there's always one way out: They should just do the right thing, and they'll be okay. It sounds simple but it's not easy to do unless you want to. So I know I did the right thing by confronting Dennis and going to the administration. That was a hard time for me but also not a hard time. I would do it again the same way.

I still don't let myself believe Dennis ever fumbled or made mistakes intentionally. To this minute, I don't think he did. But the saddest part of the whole episode is that it bounces your thoughts back to those moments and makes you wonder.

Dennis, I think, is bitter towards me, and a little bitter towards the program. He doesn't seem to feel that he did anything wrong. But I don't think he really understands the danger of betting, of how it can taint the purity of the game and the meaning of competition.

We had been outscored 157–54 over the last four games of the season. It was a dark note. Our season had kind of just fizzled out again. But it felt different than 1993. I didn't see it as squandered opportunities. I saw it as, "When we get this chance again, we're going to handle it better."

13.

The Secret Garden

"A flake of snow is very small,
'Tis lost to sight quite quickly:
But many flakes combined will fill,
The roads and pathways quickly,
United we can face the fight,
Without distress or fuss:
A little less of you or me,
A little more of us."
—William T. Card

Before our 1994 postseason banquet I spent quite a lot of time writing and compiling statements I thought would have great meaning for the team. I wanted to penetrate our players' consciousnesses before we began winter workouts, and I believed our group was fertile soil for the seeds I wanted to sow. I told them:

"A vision is just a dream until you act upon it."

"We know a person thinks, not when he tells us what he thinks, but by his actions."

"Difficulty is the one excuse that history never accepts."

"Any jackass can kick down a barn, but it takes a real carpenter to build one."

"You must do something you think you cannot do."

"Nothing splendid has ever been achieved, except by those who dared believe that something inside of them was superior to circumstances."

"The future is not something we enter, the future is something we create."

Dennis Lundy and a couple of his good friends didn't show up for our 1994 postseason banquet, so it might have seemed we didn't have all our loose ends tied up. In a way, though, that represented the beginning of tying them up.

A lot of the kids who now were finished with their eligibility were from the freshman class that I inherited. The guys I had chastised before the Iowa game were in that group, and they had been chronic problems. We had always had two or three guys who would pull the whole group down, even with little things like wanting to wear towels and tape up their shoes. They would get mad and tell me it was a cultural thing, but I didn't buy it.

They weren't bad kids, but we just were never going to be in complete harmony, and attitude and chemistry always were going to suffer because of that.

Before the Penn State game, in fact, Todd Baczek, one of our fifth-year seniors, approached me. He said, "You know, Coach, I've figured it out: I'm really going to miss next year. I'm going to miss the success you're going to have. But you know what? I know what you have to do."

I said, "What's that, Todd?"

He said, "You've got to get rid of my class. You've got to get my class and everybody in that group out."

It almost hurts to say it, and it's not meant personally, but he was right. After 1994 it was like we were purged. Talk in the locker room became infinitely more positive and the climate around the team distinctly changed. As much as I wanted it to happen earlier, though, that collective eagerness probably couldn't have come any sooner than it did.

Almost every guy now on the team had come in because of us, to be with us, and they believed in us. And we believed in them. We didn't have to test their character.

It was natural for the other guys not to quite take us to heart, which I don't blame them for. Just the same, I can't say we were doing anything radically different as coaches in 1995 than we were doing in 1994 and 1993. If we could have had the kids trusting us then I believe we could have turned the corner much sooner.

Not that we didn't still have a few wrinkles to iron out.

Rodney Ray was a fine defensive back, but he could be a pain. To his credit, he never lied or rebelled against his punishments, but he was an agitator. He was going to be a fifth-year guy and I told him I didn't want him back unless he was going to do it my way. I told him he had to be a positive force, not a negative one.

I didn't immediately renew his scholarship after spring practice. But Rodney turned around completely, and it was gratifying to see what a dedicated player he became and how he grew as a person.

And then there was the matter of Darnell.

Right after Thanksgiving I met with our returning players individually. Darnell Autry didn't come in when he was scheduled, and when he finally did show up he said he wanted a release from his scholarship so he could transfer. I asked him why. He said, "I'm not happy here, I don't fit in here and I don't want to be here."

I said, "Darnell, I'm not giving you a release. We can talk about this, we can talk about the problems, but I'm not giving you a release." He said okay, but after he left my office he had everything packed up and sent home. Then I got a call from his dad, Gene. He said, "Coach, I can't believe that if you really like this kid and care about this kid that you won't give him a release."

I said, "Gene, first of all, do you know what the consequences are even if I do give him his release? He has to sit out a year. If I don't, he has to sit out two years before he puts on a uniform and he loses a year of his eligibility."

He said, "You've got to be kidding me."

"No," I replied. He called Betsy Mosher, one of our associate A.D.s, and then called me back and said, "Okay, Coach, the penalty is too harsh."

So Darnell came back in the winter and agreed to stay through the spring and did all the things he was supposed to do. But I was skeptical and kept my eye on him.

We let the players set their goals for what they thought they needed to be able to do in order to play the next year. Then Larry Lilja set up what we called "a bowl goal," what each player needed to achieve to be part of a team that gets to a bowl. Then we gave them the "Rose Bowl goal," which was above and beyond anything they thought they could ever do. They couldn't believe how high these goals were.

In the early years even the personal goals didn't get met often because players weren't consistent about doing their workouts. Our attendance was average at best because of the constant conflict with academics. A player couldn't run today, it would go, because he had a test tomorrow, or even next week.

Even though workout sessions are considered voluntary in the winter and summer, there's no way any player can make the strength and speed improvements necessary without devoting himself at those times. So even if we can't make them do the workouts we can let them know we're watching. Before the '94 season Larry began putting a workout chart up in the weight room. If a guy didn't show, he put a red mark next to his name for that day. It was there for us to see, and for all the other guys to see, too.

In late January of '95 I asked Larry if we'd had anybody miss workouts. He said, "No, nobody's missed." I thought he was kidding, and then he said nobody had even been late. We went the entire offseason, through spring practice in March, without one player missing a workout. At Colorado, players never missed workouts, but there always seemed to be a few con artists. This was different. Larry kept saying, "This attitude is incredible."

Then spring practice came, and I'm telling you, we didn't have one bad practice. We had kids who were relieved to be there on the field only with guys who believed and were ready to win.

We simplified our offense and said, "We've got five running plays and five passing plays. That's it. Know them inside and out." We also ratcheted up our 4-3 defense after some consulting with people from the Bears, who have always been very good to us.

Mac—who had resigned at Colorado in 1994 after telling me I could always come back there!—came in to watch one day when we were just in helmets, shorts and shoulder pads. He was really tuned in to our practice, almost transfixed. He said, "Barney, I don't think I've ever seen a team practice this hard in shorts."

I stepped back and watched and thought about it, and he was right. The players had the most incredible intensity. Fantastic work habits were on display. This team was fusing together, even if it was in a virtual vacuum.

Nobody came out to watch so nobody saw any of this developing except those of us inside it. Nobody saw us coming together at the end of practice and yelling "Rose Bowl" in unison. Even if fans or reporters were watching, they probably wouldn't have been able to measure the difference like we could.

Darnell really had a heck of a spring. The first scrimmage we had was a goal line scrimmage, and he ran in there and knocked one of our safeties back about three yards. I thought, "Whoa, we've got ourselves a big-timer here."

The quarterback situation still was shaky. Lloyd Abramson hadn't been quite ready in '94 but he was dynamite with our scout team in practice. He could hum it, and the job was there for him to take. He had a death in the family in the spring, though, and missed a couple of critical days, so I couldn't immediately push him up and give him the responsibility of starting.

But we felt we pretty much knew what Steve Schnur and Tim Hughes could do from the '94 season, and they were struggling in the spring. So we made a decision to put those two guys on the shelf and force-feed Abramson and Chris Hamdorf for the last few days of the spring. There were times when Abramson was everything I thought he would be.

By the end of spring Steve probably was third, and when I met with the players individually, Steve was frustrated and really angry. We met for 30 minutes and when I went off on my run I thought, "This isn't settled. I can't live with this." I got back and had a secretary call Steve, and we met for another hour and got through some differences.

What Steve didn't know was that I was a tremendous Steve Schnur fan. He just wasn't playing consistently enough, and he simply had to be consistent to be able to lead.

After spring ball ended I got a call on the golf course from John Wristen, who told me Darnell had left. We had hooked him up with a great job at the Chicago Board of Trade, and he was supposed to start in a few days. Then Darnell's dad called me and said, "I don't want you to give him his release. He's got too much at stake, and you guys have done too much for him. Whatever you do, don't give him a release." Well, if his dad insisted, what was I going to do?

Some of our players called him and I had Rashaan Salaam of the Bears call him, too. Rashaan had tried to leave Colorado after his first year and Mac wouldn't give him his release. He won the Heisman Trophy two years later.

Finally, I called Darnell. He asked for a release and I told him again that I would listen to anything he had to say but he wasn't going to get a release. Then I said, "I know you well enough that I know you will make the right decision." He said, "Alright, Coach."

Soon after he got home to Arizona his dad kicked him out of the house. Now I was talking to his dad every day. One thing he said particularly stood out to me: "It's Father's Day coming up." Meanwhile, I found out Darnell had been to Arizona State and they had talked to him. I called their coach, Bruce Snyder, and said, "Bruce, I ain't giving this guy a release." He said, "I don't want anything to come between you and me, so I won't talk to him any more."

135

Darnell went over to his father's house on Father's Day and he finally couldn't stand for his father to feel the way he did about leaving. He came back to Evanston and went to work at the Board of Trade—and trained his fanny off the rest of the summer.

The rest is history: Darnell finished fourth in the Heisman Trophy balloting and he has to be considered a strong preseason candidate for the Heisman in 1996. It's a testament to Darnell's personality that he never seemed to lose the affection or respect of his teammates. Rob Johnson called Darnell and told him he loved him, and I remember one of our linemen said: "I'd drink molten lava for Darnell."

What I would say to Darnell after he came back was, "Remember the pump? How close were you to quitting pumping? And it all would have gone back into the bottom of the well. You pumped it one more time, and it just started to flow." From the brink of what could have been a disastrous decision, the whole world has opened up for him.

Darnell wasn't the only guy we got a job at the Board of Trade. Lloyd Abramson had one, too. On his first day of work the guy who got him the job called me and said, "There's something weird about this kid." I asked what he meant and he said, "He came down here in combat boots and a chain around his waist."

Soon after, Lloyd's mother called and said Lloyd was burnt-out. Burnt-out from work and burnt-out from football. It turned out he wasn't throwing or lifting, and around August he called and said he was quitting.

That was a real bitter pill for me to swallow but I should have seen it coming in the recruiting process. Or when he told me during his freshman year he didn't think he was ready to compete. I banked so much on him that I didn't even take a quarterback in the recruiting class behind him.

Then one of our centers, Adam Reed, called and said he wasn't coming back because things had gotten too intense academically. Adam was pre-med, and I said, "Adam, that's the way it is in pre-med." But he just said it wasn't for him. So now we'd lost probably the two best players we'd recruited in that class.

I also was worried about Hudhaifa. He was academically ineligible after the fall semester and had to enroll in junior college in the spring as well as take summer courses here.

Hudhaifa became eligible, and while the loss of Reed hurt our depth and pride a little bit, we told ourselves he wouldn't hurt our team. As for the quarterback situation, well, we just had to see which of the three guys would assert himself.

As all these things were distracting me, though, the nucleus of our team still was working out like fiends. Larry Lilja showed me a tape he'd made of the workouts.

Larry does all kinds of creative things with the running program, like taking the players down to the beach at Lake Michigan and having them run along the water where they'll fall in if they lose their balance. He'll also time the players to see how fast they can push a car around the playing field.

We really only have one hill in Evanston—Mt. Trashmore. I guess they call it that because it's made up of old trash, which is sealed in clay. Anyway, the summer of 1995 was the hottest we've had here in a long time. Emergency conditions. On the particular day that Larry filmed the players at Mt. Trashmore, it was about 103 degrees and the humidity was at its highest.

Larry planted a Rose Bowl banner at the top of the hill and filmed the guys running up and down and up and down and up. When they were done, they all collapsed around the banner. They were utterly spent, which of course was exhilarating for me to see.

Larry sent copies of that tape out to the players who hadn't stayed in Evanston, just to let them know what was up. It was contagious. When our guys reported, significantly more of them than ever before passed their conditioning tests. In fact, we had 17 guys meet their Rose Bowl goals—the ones that originally seemed impossible.

In July, we suffered a deep loss, an anguish that brought our efforts to a halt.

Marcel Price, a second-year defensive back, was shot and killed in his hometown of Nashville, Tennessee. It was horrible. The story was that a friend of his had been playing with what he thought was an empty .357 Magnum at a party. It went off and hit Marcel in the chest.

I hadn't realized how much of an impression Marcel had made on our players. I mean, every one of the 50 kids who was here that summer was shaken up. We had a grief session immediately with a priest and one of the ministers from the university. I told the kids that whoever wanted to go to the funeral, I'd find a way to get them there.

The university chartered two planes, an action I really appreciated, and we took 16 kids down to the funeral. Jerry Brown, who had recruited Marcel, and I went and it was an extremely emotional day. The funeral program described Marcel better than I can:

"He welcomed a challenge. He believed in maintaining a positive attitude and approached each obstacle with zeal. He strived to be the best by doing the best that he could. To know him was to love him—for his smile, his manner and humor—and to RESPECT his tenacity for life!! Marcel never met a stranger and he touched the lives of all who shared the joy of knowing him."

Sports Illustrated's preseason issue came out and it had us ranked 79th in the nation. Next to the ranking *SI* wrote, "Ominous sign: Wildcats' best player is punter Paul Burton."

Well, nothing against Paul Burton, but I had written a letter to our players during the summer in anticipation of the typical rash of negative preseason articles. Not necessarily negative in intent, but negative in tone, placing us last or next to last in the conference and belittling us in some way or another.

I didn't necessarily know how the articles would come out but I knew there was only one reporter who called me in the offseason to do any kind of interview. So almost anyone who was writing about us was doing it based on the spring prospectus or information from the 1994 season.

None of these reporters had any idea of what we were doing or had caught on to what we were sensing was about to happen, so I told our players not to read the magazines. I wanted their heads free and cleansed of negativity. I didn't want doubt to creep in.

I didn't read any of the articles, either. I just refused. People called and said, "Did you see what they said about you in such-and-such?" I'd say, "No," and they would say they'd send it to me. I'd just say, "You don't need to. I don't want it."

Logically, then, when we went to the Big Ten kickoff luncheon—which to me kind of marks the start of the season—none of the interviewers or questioners had an inkling that we might have a decent team. What was asked was pretty nondescript and general, the usual stuff like "Is the reason you can't do it because of the academics?" And "Do you think you'll stay in the Big Ten?"

Rob Johnson, our center, was asked about the quarterback situation and he responded, "We don't need a star quarterback. We need a quarterback who can get us in the right place and make good decisions. He doesn't need to be a star."

Rob had a great sense about that and he had told me the same thing during spring ball. He turned out to be right. That quarterback was Steve Schnur. Rob's description defines him, really.

Steve is basically an average athlete, but he's poised and intelligent and knows the offense. He earned the job with his work ethic over the summer. And once he took it he wouldn't give it up.

At the luncheon following the Big Ten press conference each coach says a few words about his team. I usually try to make mine humorous but about a week before the luncheon I still hadn't come up with what I wanted to say and I told Mary I was worried. Mary had been gardening that day, and she tried to ask me questions about the essence of the team.

Then she said, "To me, building a team is a lot like a creating a flower garden. Some flowers by themselves aren't very attractive but when you put them in with certain other flowers they blend in and seem like the perfect flower for the moment.

"Then, with perennials, it can take two or three years before they really bloom. And sometimes the wildflowers, the ones you don't count on, become the prettiest. Some flowers you have to give a lot of attention to, and some just take off by themselves."

I thought, "Wow, I've got it. This would be a great representation of our team." The analogy was right-on.

We had some guys we'd been bringing along for two or three years and they were just starting to bloom. We had some guys that if we'd move them to a different position or complement them with just the right player, they would become more productive.

Some guys we had to do a lot of work with to get ready and others we didn't have to do anything with at all. You don't just get 22 roses; and you have to make them all blend.

That became my speech. I opened it up by saying Mary had encouraged me to get in touch with my feminine side, and, as a result, I'm going to draw a comparison between our team and a flower garden.

When I left the banquet, though, my immediate thoughts were about what the other coaches had said. My head was spinning. I thought, "Man, they sounded impressive. We are going to have our hands full."

But I always leave the luncheon so pumped up, with the fresh promise of a new season just a few weeks away. As I drove back up Lake Shore Drive on this gorgeous day with all the sailboats dotting Lake Michigan, I was unbelievably excited.

Before our first 1995 season meeting with the team I reminded our coaches that we still probably weren't as talented as most of the teams we were going to be playing, and that we were the ones who could make the difference between us not being as good as anybody else and us being as good or better than everyone else. I later found out that this really gave them a surge of confidence, but I didn't do it for effect. I believed it.

At our first team meeting I presented the schedule board, as I do every year. I drew special attention to the first team on the list that we had to beat: Northwestern. We were first on the list because we hadn't been able to overcome ourselves in the past. I also talked to them about the difference between guys who play football and football players.

Then I unveiled two other boards. One contained the keys to victory, such as turnover ratio and third-down success, and the other revealed our team goals.

Normally these meetings become like seances. You ask people to talk about their goals and they stand up in the air-conditioned room and say these things and say these things, and it drones on and on and it all sounds the same.

So this time I decided I was going to tell them their goals, instead, one by one.

The first goal was the right attitude and chemistry. I was confident we were on our way to measuring up on that, but I didn't want to minimize the significance in any way.

They had to approach each practice the right way and each drill the right way and they had to understand how important each minute of each practice was. They had to trust each other and trust their coaches. Until those things happened no other steps could occur.

Our second step was to become known as a relentless team, which would be achieved when someone outside wrote about us that way or was quoted saying we were relentless. For us to think we were relentless was one thing, but for that to be another's opinion, well, I always thought that was the highest compliment you could pay a team or a player.

The third step was to achieve a winning season. The fourth step was to reach a bowl game. To have a winning season we'd obviously need six victories. To qualify for a bowl I figured we'd need seven.

The final step was the Rose Bowl. But I made it clear that I didn't want them dwelling on steps two, three, four, or five because none of those would be addressed until they met step one, attitude and chemistry, to my satisfaction.

The Notre Dame game made it seem like we had met our first goal, but the real test came in the aftermath of Miami of Ohio.

Part Three:

Run for the Roses

14.

Purple Haze

*"The difference between a successful person
and others is not a lack of strength, not a lack of
knowledge, but rather a lack of will."*
—Anonymous

After I told Mary how depressed I was feeling about the Miami of Ohio game she asked, "If you're going to act this way, how do you expect the kids to act? Who's going to show them how to act?"

She was right but I couldn't bring myself into the role yet. I had to suffer. I think part of being a coach is that when you lose you have to give yourself time to suffer, to grieve, in order to be able to truly get over it and move on.

That night Clay had a football game and I was really uncomfortable about the idea of going, because I knew I would have to sit in the stands with all these parents who had just been to our game. As it turned out I was glad I went because they were all so compassionate. They did their best to make me feel better.

I saw somebody at the game whom I had last seen at one of Clay's preseason scrimmages. Ironically enough, he was telling me during the scrimmage that I should watch the punter, and I said, "I can't watch the punter. The guy you've got to appreciate is the guy who snaps the ball." He came up to me that night and said, "I see what you were talking about."

On the news that night all the stories were, "The old Northwestern returns.... Back to reality." It was the same thing in the papers in the morning, but that's when my healing began.

In coaching, at least in our house, the game isn't really finished until you read about it in the paper the next day. You either read your obituary or you read the celebration, but either way that's the final chapter.

Sometimes when I get my mail I'll hold an envelope up to the light to see if I can figure out what's inside before I open it. It's sort of the same thing with the newspaper. It'll come in the morning and I'll maybe just set it down and casually go through the sections before I peek at sports.

It's kind of a cat-and-mouse game with myself, but ultimately I have to look at sports. The Notre Dame game was over for me when I read about it in the paper. I got up early the Sunday after the Miami game ... but it took me a while before I could make myself open to the sports section. After I read about the game it was as over as I could make it right away.

Of course it wasn't anywhere near over. Somebody said, "This, too, shall pass," but it felt like trying to pass a half-inch kidney stone. Any time you lose, under any circumstance, everything is cloudy for five or six days until you have a chance to redeem yourself. When you win, somehow every day is sunny. Because of the way our loss to Miami had happened, and after we had hit such a high with Notre Dame, this week was especially dark.

On Sunday the staff got together and had a tough time of it. It wouldn't do any good to yell, it wouldn't do any good to get upset. We just had to feel it, and hope it ran its course. Then we watched films, somberly, and did our running as a team. It was quiet. All of us seemed to be asking ourselves, "Who are we? Which team are we?"

Media attention dwindled back to normal on Monday and I remember saying, "The bandwagon is made of Teflon." Somebody told me later that was the best line I had all year. It is a good line. It certainly describes how we felt.

The next practice was Tuesday, and we were all still in a funk. We had a difficult team to prepare for, Air Force, which plays like the consummate team. We'd only beaten them 14–10 the year before, and that wouldn't have happened without Chris Martin's 96-yard fumble recovery for a touchdown.

The Falcons always are well-coached, and their Wishbone offense was unlike anything else we would see all season. Their defense also had some complications for us, so now we were going to have to change a lot of our schemes and rules. Making these major transformations was good for us, because it gave us something to concentrate on and helped us to stop brooding.

On Wednesday I called a team meeting and said it was time for us to decide what we were about. That included us, the coaches. I felt that we'd been talking the talk but I wanted to make sure we were walking the walk, too. Then I told them a story I had stumbled

144

upon in my files when I was searching for the right words. It was a story that Steve Musseau had told me years before.

There was a tribe in Africa, I told them, whose only way of surviving was by catching monkeys. They'd catch them and sell them to zoos. As the tribe's population got older it became more and more difficult to catch the monkeys.

So one of the tribesmen took a coconut and carved out a slot in the coconut that would be just big enough for a monkey to slide his hand into. They knew the monkeys liked to come into camp and raid for crackers and cookies, and they knew they were particularly fond of Oreo cookies. They put an Oreo in the coconut, attached the coconut to a chain and the chain to a tree. They set up 15 of these contraptions.

The next morning, sure enough, there were 15 monkeys caught in the coconuts. The hole was just big enough for the monkey to slide in an open hand and grab the Oreo. But the hole wasn't big enough for him to pull his hand, in a fist around the Oreo, back out.

It was an obvious analogy, I thought. The monkeys were trapped because they couldn't let go of the cookie. I said, "Miami of Ohio is our cookie, and if we don't let go of it, we're done. We're trapped. We're never going to get away from it."

Did that story make a difference? Did it turn our light back on? I sort of think so. The guys seemed kind of relieved, and we had a good practice that day. To tell you the truth, I don't think we ever talked about Miami again after that unless somebody else brought it up.

Beyond cleansing ourselves of Miami we had to get emotionally ready to play Air Force. The difference might seem subtle but I thought they were two distinct matters.

As it happened we found a few sources of motivation. Somebody sent us an article out of a Colorado newspaper quoting an Air Force player saying, "Somebody's going to have to pay for what happened last year," and "Paybacks are a bitch." We put that in everybody's itinerary.

On Thursday we gave the players the *Sun-Times*' "Do You Believe in Miracles?" T-shirts—embellished with our own words on the back: "This Was No Damn Miracle." I recently read an article in my fraternity magazine that quoted Sam Valenzisi, our kicker, saying, "I'll always remember that. It was as though he had given us back our swagger."

I thought it also was an appropriate time to address the team goal board again, and I pointed to this game as the litmus test of our attitude and chemistry. I said we were going to find out right now if we had it. The Air Force game was our chance to establish it and move on to the next goal.

We did one other thing on Thursday. For away games we help the players prepare for an unfriendly crowd by playing over the Dyche loudspeaker a recording of crowd noises. The recording must have been made in the 1950s and it's filled with kind of corny stuff like "Hold that line," and "Block that kick." We warn everybody in the neighborhood each week when we do that.

This was the Thursday before a home game, though, so we wouldn't ordinarily use the sound system. But I had a surprise in mind. As the players were stretching I decided I was going to try to recapture the emotion of Kenosha. I was watching the guys carefully when over the loudspeaker, full blast, came this, "Da, Da, Da ..." It was "High Hopes."

You could just see these huge grins come over every face. This melancholy group of guys who didn't know who they were—myself included—seemed to transform right there in front of me. With all the noise from the loudspeaker and the singing, people came drifting out of our academic center to see what in the world was going on.

The song hit a chord, and athletes are superstitious. So about the same time the next Thursday, before the Indiana game, Rob Johnson looked up at me as they lined up to stretch and asked, "Well?"

The song came on just as he finished saying that, and we played it every Thursday thereafter. Before long, the media were coming out to see this spectacle of 100 guys singing "High Hopes."

We entered the Air Force game mired in a 0-10-1 streak at home; we had only won three times at Dyche since I came in 1992. But I felt reassured about our state of mind by game time.

Still, we couldn't avoid some doubt creeping in after our experience with Miami. To fend off doubt, I thought there was one certain command to give: Play hard. Play 60 minutes. That's all I tried to convey before the game: "You saw what happened when you didn't play hard for four quarters."

No one took the risk again. Darnell rushed 37 times for 190 yards and our defense refused to let Air Force into the end zone. Pat Fitzgerald had an interception and a fumble recovery and was co–Big Ten defensive player of the week. He won it three times last season and our players began referring to the honor as "The Pat Fitzgerald Award." Fitz went on to be the Big Ten Defensive Player of the Year.

We tried to have a little ingenuity as coaches, too. We ran a fake field goal that didn't work but we successfully executed a fake punt and an onside kick. We wanted to reaffirm that our special teams were an asset. We won 30–6.

Given our loss to Miami of Ohio, it probably was harder for us to beat Air Force than it was to beat Notre Dame. We all let out a deep breath of relief. We had regained some equilibrium.

Now we were into the Big Ten season, beginning with Indiana. We had some confidence about playing the Hoosiers since we had beaten them at their place in 1994. We had no idea how good we were, but we were back to having confidence that we were at least good.

When we met early that week, I told the team we had achieved Goal No. 1: We had become a team with great attitude and great chemistry. Now it was time for us to move on and become a relentless team.

I went out for my run the morning of the game, and as I passed a guy who was out walking, he looked me in the eye and said, "Go get 'em, Coach." When I talked to the team that morning, I told them about that and I said, "You know, it really comes down to this." I hit my hand on the table and yelled, "Go get 'em!" It jolted everybody. I didn't have to say anything after that.

We won 31–7, but before our defense clamped them down it was only 10–7 at halftime. It was one of five times our D would shut out the opponent in the second half, a contrast from years past when we could stay with a team for a half before we'd just dissolve. The difference? A combination of maturity, conditioning and confidence.

Our offense purred, too, with Darnell breaking 100 yards for the fifth straight time since he started against Penn State the year before. Our special teams really were special and got us going: Paul Burton had a 90-yard punt—with the help of a couple hops—that kept Indiana off-balance, and Brian Musso had an 86-yard punt return that set up a touchdown by Darnell. Valenzisi kicked three field goals, too.

Indiana sustained a major loss in the third quarter, when their excellent running back Alex Smith suffered broken ribs. He stayed in the hospital overnight and I visited him the next morning and told him what a great player I thought he was. He had already rushed for about 140 yards when he got hurt and we were having trouble containing him. They really couldn't do anything after he came out.

Still, I wouldn't say we established authority over the game until Casey Dailey returned a fumble 43 yards for a touchdown early in the fourth quarter. That made it 28–7, the same lead we had had over Miami of Ohio. But our guys weren't going to let that score create déjà vu.

The one disappointing thing about the game was that we only had 29,000 people at Dyche. We had entered the game 2–1 with a victory over Notre Dame, and I thought we might have merited more attention and support. But I think linebacker Casey Dailey pointed out that "the bear" had been on our back for 24 years, and that it was just going to take some time to get rid of it.

Our confidence was bubbling now. It was only the sixth Big Ten victory in my four seasons and it was the first time we had beaten anybody in the conference by more than two touchdowns—and we viewed Indiana as a tough program.

We were 3–1, Northwestern's best start since 1963, but we weren't pleased. We knew we should have been 4–0. But at least that knowledge was working to our advantage.

Coach Gary Barnett is all smiles after defeating highly favored Notre Dame in the opening game of the 1995 season. *(photo by Jonathan Daniel)*

Barnett's high school football coach, Jack Wells. *(courtesy of Wells family)*

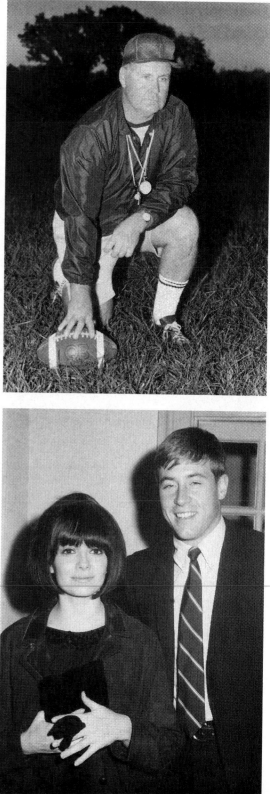

Gary and future wife Mary getting ready to attend their high school prom. *(courtesy of Barnett personal collection)*

Gary and Mary at the 1967 University of Missouri Beta Theta Pi Christmas formal. *(courtesy of Barnett personal collection)*

Barnett (right) with his mentor, former University of Colorado head football coach Bill McCartney. *(courtesy of Barnett personal collection)*

Northwestern University 1995 football training camp at Kenosha. *(photo by Jonathan Daniel)*

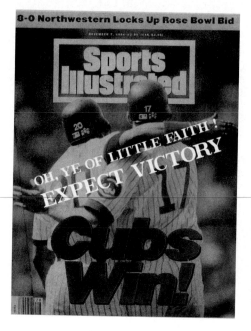

Oh, ye of little faith. In a 1994 issue of *Sports Illustrated*, the magazine had a laugh at Northwestern's expense when it predicted the Wildcat's chances of playing in the Rose Bowl were as likely as the Cubs winning the World Series. *(photo by Stephen Green)*

Darnell Autry breaks into the open field against USC in the Rose Bowl. *(photo by Chris Covatta)*

Coach Barnett meets with the press after defeating Purdue 23–8. *(photo by Jonathan Daniel)*

Autry scoring a touchdown became a familiar sight during the 1995 season. Here he crosses the goal line against Penn State. *(photo by Jonathan Daniel)*

Linebacker Pat Fitzgerald, the heart and soul of the Northwestern defense. *(photo by Jonathan Daniel)*

The opportunistic Northwestern defense forces a fumble against Wisconsin.
(*photo by Jonathan Daniel*)

1995 Big Ten Champions. *(courtesy of Northwestern University)*

15.

The Eagle Has Landed

"Once you are moving in the direction
of your goals ... nothing can stop you."
—Anonymous

After the Indiana game I was given an article from the Louisville paper that said we were "relentless." The kids went crazy when I told them about it. Now we could aim at Goal No. 3: a winning season.

Michigan was up next for us and somebody remarked to me, "You're playing with the big boys, huh?"

I said, "No, we are the big boys."

I wasn't going to let my guard down or compromise on those types of belittling statements. Part of our faith and belief in ourselves depended on not tolerating that kind of thinking. Trouble was, I could tell our players were a little uptight, maybe a little awe-struck by what we had been doing.

We were ranked 25th going into the game and Michigan was No. 7 and 5–0. Michigan is a special, special place to play, with more than 100,000 people at every game. None of us had ever coached in that stadium, and only one player on our team had even been in there. So our audio-visual people put together some highlights, including shots of the full house in the Michigan stands, the band, and all the pageantry, and we set it to Michigan's fight song, "Hail to the Victors."

"First of all," I told the team, "I want you to know what you're getting into, okay? Let's just get used to it right now." I wanted them to have been there; I wanted them to feel like it was familiar territory. Then I gave out our scouting report on Michigan, and the theme was, "Eagle or Oyster?"

"When God made the oyster," the report started, "He guaranteed its absolute economic and social security. He built the oyster a house, its shell, to shelter and protect it from enemies. When hungry, the oyster simply opens its shell and food rushes in. The oyster has freedom from want.

"But when God made the eagle he declared, 'The blue sky is the limit; build your own house!' So the eagle built on the highest mountain that storms threaten every day. For food, the eagle flies through miles of rain and snow and wind. The eagle, not the oyster, is the symbol of America."

Then I said, "You know that Michigan is the oyster. Michigan doesn't have to struggle for anything. They open their mouths, and recruits come. We are the eagle. We're the ones who struggle. We're the ones who don't have an indoor facility to practice in. We're the ones who have had to meet all the adversities."

Since there was almost a tangible tension among the players, I tried to lighten things up a little, too. So I put together a little dialogue with our trainer, Steve Willard.

"You know, I'm really worried about this Michigan team," I said, "so I had Steve call the Michigan trainer."

Steve stood up, and I said, "Steve, did you call the Michigan trainer?" He answered, "Yeah, Coach."

"What did you find out?" I asked.

"Coach," he said, "every player on the Michigan team has a navel."

I said, "Oh, no, you're kidding me!"

Steve said, "No, Coach, every one of them." The kids were looking at us like, "Where are you possibly going with this?"

Then I asked, "Steve, how many guys on our team have navels?"

"Coach, every one of them," Steve replied.

"Whew, what a relief," I said, and then I sent the players out of the room.

It was just my way of trying to break the ice a bit and saying, "Hey, there isn't any difference here." I always try to get them to see that. For instance, I'll take the All-American teams and compare the size of our players to the size of the All-Americans. And I'll just say, "What is the difference? Your height's almost the same, your weight's almost the same, your speed's almost the same, your bench press is almost the same, your vertical leap's almost the same.

"Why is he a better player? What makes him a better player than you? Maybe he isn't, but why is he perceived as a better player? Obviously, it isn't anything physical. Why aren't you an All-American? Why aren't you playing at that level? What's going to keep you from playing at that level?"

150

* * *

Still, when we looked at Michigan, man, were they loaded. The Wolverines had opened the season with a stunning comeback against Virginia. They had just gotten better and better and better since then although there was one encouraging thing we saw in the films:

Michigan had led Miami of Ohio 31–0 and Miami almost did the same thing to the Wolverines that it did to us. The final was 38–19 but it might have been 31–26 at one point if not for a controversial interception call. Seeing that was a bit of a relief because of what it said about both those teams. It consoled us, sort of, about what had happened to us with Miami, and it made us see Michigan as mortal despite its tremendous talent.

Michigan's defense might have been the best I'd seen in the Big Ten. Extremely physical. We thought we would need a couple of surprises in our offensive arsenal to keep them off-balance, or at least honest, so we put in a trick play as part of our game plan.

On defense, I didn't feel like they could beat us in the air. I was worried, though, that they would just keep giving the ball to Tim Biakabutuka. The message I wanted our defense to get was that if we could keep it tight into the fourth quarter, we would frustrate them and win.

At the beginning of the game, we fell behind 6–0, but Sam Valenzisi kicked two field goals—the second with one second left in the first half—to tie it. We hadn't slowed down Biakabutuka a lick, although we had a nice goal line stand to force one of their field goals.

Michigan executed a beautiful drive early in the third quarter and went ahead 13–6 on Brian Griese's bootleg run. Even though replays seemed to show he was down before he got in, it was clear they weren't having much trouble with our defense.

But Sam kicked another field goal to keep it close and Eric Collier came up with a huge interception early in the fourth quarter by hanging back and lulling Griese to sleep. It was time for the gadget play.

On first down at the Michigan 35 Schnur lateraled to D'Wayne Bates, whom we originally recruited as a quarterback. D'Wayne threw a perfect pass to Darren Drexler, our tight end. First and goal. Two plays later Schnur threw a two-yard touchdown pass to our fullback, Matt Hartl.

Fitz sacked Griese on their next series and momentum was with us. Sam made another field goal and it was 19–13. Biakabutuka, who finished with more than 200 yards, ran Michigan to around our 30 with two minutes left, but then the Wolverines decided to throw and got themselves into a fourth-and-long predicament. William Bennett intercepted, and we ran out the clock.

I remember William saying afterward what a beautiful noise it was to hear 100,000 people be so quiet.

I hadn't ordered the guys not to carry me off the field, but nobody tried to. I do, however, confess to briefly dancing with Rob Johnson on the field. It just kind of came over me. We had played valiantly and gallantly, and I thought Michigan was the best team we were going to play all season. We were fortunate to win, and if we had played 10 games last year, I'm not sure Michigan wouldn't have won nine.

But on that day, it was ours. I told the guys, "The eagle has landed."

From the feeling on the field during the game, the Michigan coaches and players had been relatively sure this wasn't going to be much of a game. And there had been some bad blood between our staffs ever since we first met in '92. But at Missouri I had played with Lloyd Carr, their interim coach, and he was a gentleman after the game.

Yet the thing I remember most is the classy way their fans behaved. They tipped their caps and waved to us as we left the stadium, and I was moved. I did not anticipate that at all.

After working for Mac for eight years, everything you heard was about the Michigan way because of the time he'd spent there under Bo Schembechler. Between that and our initial dealings with them, I have to admit I'd probably built up a little resentment. This game gave me an appreciation for Michigan, and reminded me that in a lot of ways I'm somewhat a product of the school myself because of Mac.

The win was monumental for our program. No one could suggest any longer that winning at Notre Dame was a fluke. We had to be the real deal. I don't know how anybody could question our legitimacy—and from what I saw on the way home, nobody was questioning us about anything. It became a wild scene. Bonkers. Even our police escorts were using purple lights. They cleared out all of Central Street for our return.

Part of the fun for us was that N.U.M.B.—otherwise known as the Northwestern University Marching Band—had made the trip with us. We share a special relationship with the band. I once did a promotion for the band where I dressed up in a band uniform and did a spinoff of "Uncle Sam Wants You" as a recruiting poster for them.

That was my daughter Courtney's freshman year at Northwestern and the posters were all over campus. She said every hallway she entered had a picture of me pointing at her. She was seeing more of me than ever.

John Paynter, our legendary band director, got run over by Darnell during the Michigan game. Darnell got up and asked, "Are you alright?" John said, "Don't worry about me—get back in there and score a touchdown."

I teased John after the Notre Dame game, because I thought he had been exaggerating when he had said the win was the greatest moment of his life. He died shortly after the season, but his wife said it was with a smile on his face because of our getting to the Rose Bowl.

At home following the Michigan game, the phone was ringing off the hook. I think the same pizza man came back again, too. Some of our coaches smoked cigars that night—as they should have. Our back porch was covered with cigar butts.

Mac called and he said, "I don't believe it, Barney. Do you know what you've done?" Then he said, "You've probably gotten Lloyd fired." But Lloyd Carr did a great job all season and got the fulltime job.

We moved up 11 spots in the rankings the next day and since we were 2–0 in the conference and alone in first place—in front of five teams by a half-game—people were daring to mention the Rose Bowl.

Uh-uh. As much as I didn't want us polluted by negativity, I also didn't want us to lose our focus. I wasn't going to talk about any bowl game yet. We had to achieve a winning season before I'd even mention it.

I thought discussing bowl possibilities at that point would be like letting water into a crack in a rock. If the water freezes, the rock will break up. So I told reporters I was going to try to hermetically seal the players' brains from those dangerous thoughts.

In hindsight, though, I know I slipped up once or twice in that regard. It turns out that before the Michigan game, I casually made a reference that was uncharacteristically ahead of myself:

"Keep in mind," I said to the players, "you're probably going to have to beat Michigan to go to the Rose Bowl."

16.

Eye of the Wolf

"I'm just a plowhand from Arkansas,
but I have learned how to hold a team together. You
have to lift some up, and calm others down, until
finally they've got one heartbeat together. That's
all it takes to get people to win."
—Bear Bryant

Nobody on our team had ever been 4–1, or won three games in a row before. This was a new experience, but not altogether foreign.

In 1994 we had been 3-3-1 and had real visions of a winning season but we didn't open the door. I think that the experiences then of letting opportunities pass by helped us learn how to take advantage of them now.

Minnesota was our next opponent, another team with an excellent back, Chris Darkins. Minnesota's coach, Jim Wacker, is a great guy and a real friend, but he gave us something to work with that week. At one of his press conferences he was recorded saying, "I expect to beat Northwestern, and I expect us to be ranked in the Top 25 as a result."

What he said wasn't anything I wouldn't have said to my own team, but to me it was fair game for building a cause, building urgency. I played that recording a couple times for our guys.

Also, a Minnesota columnist named Sid Hartman wrote that Northwestern must have changed its admission standards, which really upset me and helped me build the cause even further.

Sometime during that week somebody sent me a beautiful postcard of a wolf. The first thing that comes to mind when I think of a wolf is its eyes. They're clear, menacing. They almost seem to be looking through you, and the wolf never blinks. Larry Lilja had told me that wolves have been known to stalk their prey for 11 miles without taking their eyes off them.

I thought, "Wow, that's a look and a feeling I want us to have." I put that postcard up on the overhead in front of the team and said, "This is what we must be. We have to take on the eye of the wolf. When he stalks you he never takes his eye off you. And he stalks, and stalks, and stalks. The minute you look away ..."

I warned Sam Valenzisi that I was going to demonstrate on him so I approached him and stared into his eyes. When he finally glanced away, I lunged at him. It had a startling effect and I reminded our guys that wolves hunt in packs. If we had to stalk Minnesota for 11 miles, well, we were going to stalk them for 11 miles.

Because of the way our schedule had worked out this was the second year in a row we were playing at Minnesota. This actually didn't bother us because we had enjoyed the atmosphere at the Metrodome the year before. It's helpful having the replay board right there; you get to see exactly what happened and in some cases it allows you to make adjustments on the spot.

We fell behind 14–3 and I blame myself for a punt we had blocked when we were trying to set up a fake. The next time we got the ball we had to punt again. Paul Burton hit an enormous shot, though, and Minnesota fumbled to set up a score for us. By halftime we had tied it 14–14.

We had thrown an interception at the goal line in the first half and at halftime I really got on Greg Meyer's case. Chris Hamdorf was in the game because Schnur had been shaken up, and I thought Greg's play call was unfair to Chris because he hadn't thrown a pass under such tight conditions. It was one of the few times I got upset with anybody all year, and as usual when I behave like that, it was later clear to me I was wrong.

Greg calls the plays and he doesn't need any help or interference from me. In fact, I try hard to keep out of the way. I don't even usually wear a headset on the sidelines, except early in the season. I just get to a point where I'm calm and confident in what my guys are doing, and I don't want to get in their way. If they want me they know where to reach me.

After a few games they have a feel for what I like, too, and I think it's a pretty fluid operation. Most of what we do is scripted to the situation during the week, anyway. So if I knew the plan and agreed to it in a calm, analytical situation during the week, why should I suddenly disagree with it under duress?

Darnell Autry scored his second and third touchdowns of the game to give us a 27–14 lead, and we won 27–17. Darnell finished with 169 yards. The most amazing statistic, though, was that he fumbled. It was his only fumble all season—in nearly 400 carries.

I really felt bad for Coach Wacker after the game because they had played hard and hit hard and had a chance to beat us. I hoped he wasn't too down. He's taken a lot of heat because the program is struggling. I went over to Minnesota's locker room and, in fact, talked to him while he was in the shower.

The game wasn't elegant, and we probably played more like alley cats than wolves. But we haven't yet gotten caught up in having to win by a certain number of points to relish a victory.

After I finished my press conference, I said, "Now, where's Sid Hartman?" It turned out he had just left but I said, "I want it known that I thought that was irresponsible journalism. He had no right to say that, he had no data and he is dead-wrong."

Sid later caught wind of my comments and wrote me a letter of apology. I called and thanked him.

We were 5–1 now and had scooted up to 11th in the poll but the nature of the questions we were getting led me to realize people still saw us as a "Cinderella" that was going to expire at midnight. They figured that sooner or later the glass slipper was coming off.

Wisconsin was next, and I still ached over how the Badgers had shredded us in 1994. Other than Miami of Ohio, that probably was the hardest loss I've ever been associated with.

By now people at least wanted to come watch us play. Word was the game would sell out and we'd have about 50,000 people at Dyche. That hadn't happened since 1983 so I didn't care that half the people probably would be Wisconsin fans.

The kids had really been looking forward to this game. Our practices that week were as good as they've been and late in the week I just wanted to make sure they kept moving in the direction they were heading. On my run, though, a very logical theme came to me:

Big Six. It was so obvious I couldn't believe I hadn't thought of it sooner. Our sixth win would give us the first winning season since 1971. Big Six: Marcel. That was the nickname he had given himself after wearing that number in high school. I had "Big Six" put on the cover of the itinerary and when I gave it to the coaches one of them said his heart was in his throat. When we gave it to the kids in the Thursday night meeting they were obviously moved.

157

Before the game I reminded them again to choose one play and play it for Marcel. Well they must have each played 30 plays for Marcel. They were obsessed and the crowd was ours. Our theme in chapel that morning had been the difference between risk-taking and chances, and we didn't take any chances: From the minute the game started, Wisconsin was not going to win.

The Badgers fumbled a punt and a kickoff. They had a guy catch a pass and try to put on a move—only for the ball to inexplicably pop out of his arms right to us. I was standing on the sideline next to Tom Brattan, and he said, "I've never seen anything like this in my life." It was like Marcel was out there grabbing this ball here, that ball there. Wisconsin turned it over seven times.

There wasn't anything their coach, Barry Alvarez, could do. I've been there before. Barry's a good friend, and I would never have wished that on him.

But, of course, I was glad it happened. My endorphins ran rampant. Off the charts. We won 35-0—for Northwestern's first shutout since 1986. Cinderella? Didn't look like it to me.

The game wasn't without a loss for us, though. Sam Valenzisi, whose school-record streak of 13 consecutive successful field goal attempts had come to an end that day, was injured and out for the season. Sam had pretty well established himself as an All-American by then.

We had taken him out earlier to give Brian Gowins some practice but Brian had struggled so we put Sam back in for the last kickoff. Sam hit this knuckleball, and Wisconsin's returner had to fall on it deep in Badger territory. Sam saw that, jumped up in the air to celebrate, came down on his flat leg ... and tore his anterior cruciate ligament.

Emotion is such a major part of the game and sometimes it's hard to convince kids of the right times and places to let go. Usually, we try to be businesslike, but Sam is an emotional person. It was an unbelievable way to lose a player. Freaky.

Sam, though, wasn't done contributing. For one thing, he took responsibility for Brian, and it really helped. For another, he could still talk ... and talk ... and talk. Sam is spirited and articulate—and verbose. He was the master of ceremonies at our post-season banquet.

When we reviewed the game film we saw that Darnell had scored on a swing pass that really was thrown backwards. It was a good two yards backwards, so it actually was a lateral. Which counts as a rushing attempt. So the play should have been counted as a run. Without that 32-yard run Darnell had less than 100 yards for the first time.

I didn't know how to handle this so I called our sports information people over. I said, "Now, look at this play and score it as you see it. However you see it is how it goes." They looked at the film and said, "Well, it's a lateral." I said, "Okay. So do we try to change it, or not?" They called the NCAA and had it changed and Darnell's streak was intact.

There seemed to be a little controversy over what happened. But the truth is the matter didn't really concern me and I don't think Darnell or anybody else was concerned about it. I just wanted to do the right and fair thing. We do that every week with our own records of tackles. After a game we review the stats with the more precise benefit of film and slow-motion and make any corrections.

We had met goal No. 3; and now we could address exclusively goal No. 4: a bowl game. In some circumstances winning six games actually might have secured our goal. But nobody wanted to leave any margin for error, and the kids were convinced we needed a seventh win to qualify for a bowl.

I had complete confidence in the team's attitude, and it was clear to me how much the Miami game still was insulating us from any sense of complacency. It made us keenly able to play one game at a time, clichéd as that sounds. The guys had a great ability to concentrate on what was right before them and not get caught up in either what they already had done or what lay ahead.

Our next game was against Illinois, which I consider a natural rivalry because of the number of kids we get from the state. I've heard Lou Tepper say we probably consider this game more of a rivalry than they do, and I believe that. Still, it's the one game we actually play for a trophy: the Sweet Sioux Tomahawk.

Coach Tepper, Ron Vanderlinden, and I went way back—to our days at Colorado. When I first got to Boulder, I knew the city's reputation for being pretty wild. So when I went into Lou's office the first time and saw him putting a needle in his arm, I thought, "Oh, my God, what have I gotten into?" It turned out Lou is diabetic. After I got over my surprise we became close and roomed together on the road for a while.

Vandy really is a product of Lou in a lot of ways, since he coached for Lou when Lou was defensive coordinator at C.U.

When we first arrived here I had to encourage him to cut loose of Lou's influence and create his own mold. I wanted Vandy to know that I had faith in him, and that faith has been rewarded many times since.

Illinois had two splendid linebackers, Simeon Rice and Kevin Hardy, but the Illini had had quite a bit of difficulty producing points. Lou has had some trouble keeping offensive coordinators, and that's made it hard for them to be consistent.

Overall, though, we knew the Illini were talented and well-coached and had a lot going for them. And they also had two weeks to prepare for us.

The night before the game we followed our typical road-game routine, part of which means we want everything to feel as much like home as possible. We usually practice in Evanston on Friday and then have our meetings and video tests. We put the kids under the gun with our offensive and defensive schemes. For example, in our offensive meeting we'll put an image on the screen of a particular defense we might see. We'll call out the play and then every guy, one by one, has to call out his assignment. It's a good way to hold them accountable for the game plan.

Then we eat dinner and around seven get on a bus, or flight, as the case may be. In this instance, we got to the hotel in Champaign around 9:30, grabbed a snack, and had the kids in their rooms around 10:30.

It was homecoming at Illinois, which was nothing new for us. Every year we get to see more homecoming queens than anybody in the Big Ten. I not only get to see Northwestern's, I usually get to see three or four others since the schools have reasoned, fairly enough given our past, that the occasion might be enhanced by our presence.

Early in the game, it didn't look like we'd disappoint their crowd. Illinois threw a defense at us we could never have predicted, and they caught a nice break on a deflected pass that set them up to go ahead 14–0. It looked like it could get ugly.

Some people had anticipated that we might go into the tank coming off our win over Wisconsin. But despite the start against Illinois we remained patient and purposeful, signs of our maturity. Brian Gowins, who was a second-year freshman, kicked a 49-yard field goal right after Illinois' second touchdown. Then D'Wayne Bates defied a stiff wind to make a great catch and it was 14–10 at halftime.

D'Wayne had more to do with that play than just the catch: He had told us that he could run by his guy in the coverage, which he really shouldn't have been able to do but managed to do anyway.

It was drizzling and dark all day even though we began the game at 11:30 A.M. And the wind, gusting up to 25 miles per hour, was a major factor. At halftime, I decided we just had to have the wind in our favor in the fourth quarter.

This was a critical decision so I approached our defense. I said, "I've got to know how you feel about holding them, because I think we've got to give them the wind in the third quarter—so they'll have the wind and the ball. I've got to know whether we really feel good that we can stop them in the third quarter."

To a man, they said they could.

Illinois got some pretty decent field position to work with in the third quarter but our defense kept them out of the end zone for the period—as well as for the rest of the game. We had tinkered with our blocking schemes at halftime, but we still couldn't move the ball. I was looking forward to getting the ball with the wind in the fourth quarter.

When we did, we had a beautiful six-minute drive from our own 42 after Illinois had to punt into the wind. On fourth and goal, Darnell scored with 6:14 left—with a big assist from Steve Schnur. Against Wisconsin, we had used a quarterback sneak on fourth and goal and didn't get in, but here we were tempted to use that play again. During the timeout Schnur insisted that it wouldn't work. We went with Steve's alternative, a toss sweep, and we were ahead 17–14.

Illlinois ended the game having to heave a Hail Mary from about 40 yards away, and Eric Collier made a great interception to keep it from Illinois' Jason Dulick. Game over.

We were 7–1, Northwestern's best record since the last Big Ten championship in 1936, and we were assured of going to a bowl game for the first time since 1949. After all the hooting and hollering in the locker room—which included a rousing rendition of our fight song, which we hadn't had to know real well in years past—I told the guys we'd be going somewhere warm for Christmas.

It was safe to talk about it now: Reaching the Rose Bowl was the remaining goal in our pyramid.

After the Illinois game we had gone from No. 8 to No. 6 in the nation and I got pretty bold. Penn State, Iowa, and Purdue remained in front of us and I just told the guys, "It looks to me like we ought to run the table." I mean, I thought we were pretty good.

17.

Letting Go

*"Man is so made that whenever
anything fires his soul, impossibilities vanish."*
—Jean de la Fontaine

Even if we won all of our remaining games we weren't assured of going to the Rose Bowl. Ohio State still was undefeated and, according to the Big Ten tie-breaker rules, the Buckeyes would get the Rose Bowl if they won the rest of their games. A lot of people thought it was a shame that Ohio State wasn't on our schedule this season but I never dwelled on that.

We had no control over Ohio State but we couldn't let that distract us. All I knew was that we were in control of our own actions. And who knew? Ohio State might slip up somewhere.

If not, we would have the honor and reward of being conference co-champions, knowing we did all we could to make the Buckeyes earn their way to the Rose Bowl—and we'd have the opportunity to play in another prominent bowl game. If the Buckeyes did slip it would be in conference play and would put them behind us and us in the Rose Bowl.

In the back of my mind I felt Michigan would be an extreme chore for the Buckeyes in their last game. But we didn't address any of that with the team. It was at best speculation, at worst fantasy, and had no bearing on what we needed to be and do.

Champions are crowned in November, I told the team. People forget what you did in September and what you did in October. I reminded the guys, too, that they'd beaten Notre Dame in the first week of September and beaten Michigan in the first week of October. So it would be appropriate for us to follow up by beating an excellent team like Penn State in the first week of November.

Oddsmakers favored Penn State to win by almost a touchdown but I don't think we had been favored to win once all season. Not

163

only would nobody bet on us—which suited me in more ways than one—but we still had people making fun of us.

That week we got ahold of some nonsense that had been in a publication at Penn State. When I put this on our overhead, I'm telling you, the steam just went right up through our roof.

"Once upon a time," it went, "long, long ago in a faraway land, there was a rough and tumble bunch of young men who formed a team to play a game that they decided to call football. Twenty-two of them gathered, and they practiced until they got pretty good. They spread the news far and wide across the land.

"Others took notice of the game and decided they would give it a try, too. So, everywhere teams of 22 sprang up and they practiced and practiced and they turned out pretty good, too. Those teams ... formed leagues and played against each other, keeping scores and standings along the way.

"But there was one team that just wasn't any good. Oh, sure, they had their moments. But they were so few and far between ... They kept playing, and one year, wouldn't you know, they won. They were winners. They were beating teams that had for the longest time beaten them, and they were in first place in their conference.

"Everyone was happy and pulling for their team because it was their season. Finally, from the rubble, they had built a solid contender for the title ... And then one Saturday, a team that had been good since the dawn of time came in and beat the crap out of them. Prediction: Penn State 31, Northwestern 19."

This story reminds me of one guy who was always hammering and ridiculing us: ESPN's Lee Corso, who used to coach Indiana. He just seems to have this thing about Northwestern never having a chance. Maybe his critical approach to us in 1995 was a hangover from a running battle I'd had with him over the years.

There's a local radio show with a theme of "Who you crappin'?" People call in and say stuff like "What was this coach thinking? Who's he crappin'?" So at one of the Big Ten luncheons, I stood up in front of 2,000 people and said, "Let me give you Lee's coaching record over the years [41-68-2 at Indiana].... I can take it from people who've been successful. But I don't have to take it from Lee Corso. 'Lee Corso, who you crappin'?' "

The radio station still plays that constantly. I have to say, it was a pretty good promo.

Against Penn State, however, we had the real deal in broadcasting coming to town: Keith Jackson. He is gracious and eloquent and it was an honor to know that he would be presiding over the game.

I met with the seniors that Thursday morning as I always do. It's their time to tell me what's going on with the team and what they think I need to do. I said, "Men, what do you want me to do from here?" They basically said, "Don't worry, Coach. This game can't get here soon enough." They meant it, and I knew it.

Penn State had embarrassed us in 1994. Like Boston College in 1992, it was our fault, not the other team's. But we had been embarrassed and were planning to atone. I never even had to say a word about 1994, though. It was perhaps the easiest game I ever had to prepare us for emotionally.

That weekly meeting with seniors is a leadership breakfast and each week I go through phases of leadership with them. The cover page of the handout I give them says, "Leaders are like eagles. They don't flock. You find them one at a time."

The substance of what I use comes from the teachings of a Northwestern professor, Robert P. Neuschel of the Kellogg Graduate School of Management. One of our graduate assistants took his class in 1992 and shared Professor Neuschel's work with me. I understand that he is considering expanding these thoughts into a book about what he calls the need for the "servant leader."

His words from the 1992 course embody concepts I practice, believe in, and aspire to. Here are a few I find particularly meaningful.

—It is not the lot of the leader to be served but rather his/her privilege to serve. "Ich Dien" appears prominently on the crest of the Prince of Wales. It says so simply, "I Serve." Putting that concept into practice is the basis for developing the servant leader concept.

—The effective leader is mentally and emotionally grown up. He has matured—is objective and thoughtful. Such a leader must be free of arrogance and moodiness and realistically well-adjusted to life.

—The leader must have a high tolerance for ambiguity and learn to live and be productive in an increasingly uncertain environment. The managerial playing field will be messy and require a great deal of sorting out and striving to operate on an even keel in an ever-changing and churning sea.

—The leader needs unswerving strength of character. The choices will be difficult. The temptations many. Making the right decisions will not be so much intellectual as demanding of one's character.

—Many great military commanders were as natural as children—

165

straightforward—not artful—no acting—no pretense. Naturalness is a priceless virtue in leadership.

—You have to be able to say "yes" or "no" crisply. Don't waffle. You can withhold a decision but do not be or appear to be tentative in the process.

Professor Neuschel since has reworked and expanded on some of his philosophies. Here are a few of his latest intriguing thoughts:

—Plato in the fifth century B.C. gave us a credo that lays the basis for the "servant leader" when he said, "We govern for the benefit of the governed." I paraphrase that to say, "We lead for the benefit of the led."

—Strong leaders do not nibble around the edges. They don't dabble with minutiae. Charles DeGaulle said it more poetically than I: "Big people do not splash about in shallow water...."

—The leader must never be mean or small. Arrogance after a breach of integrity is the cardinal leadership sin.

—The meaningful image of the genuine leader is not just a surface picture at some instant in time. Rather it is an honest reflection of the leaders' values demonstrated over a period of time.... In brief, he/she lives these quality values which are a genuine reflection of the true inner person.

The atmosphere at Dyche was nothing less than spectacular for the Penn State game. It was a sellout again but for the first time the stands were dominated by purple. People were tailgating at the lake. We had trouble getting our bus to the stadium, not because our escort wasn't a priority but because of the parking situation. We had never seen anything like it. Marcel's parents were at the game, too.

It no longer made any difference how miserable our facilities were, how much we'd had to go through, how much difficulty people in the stands had getting into a restroom or finding something to eat. The lights were on, Keith Jackson was doing the game, and No. 6 Northwestern was playing No. 12 Penn State.

As we warmed up, a couple of my coaches came in and said Joe Paterno, the Penn State coach, was looking for me. When I got out to him, Joe shook my hand and said, "I've got one piece of advice for you: Get all you can. Demand everything, and get all you can."

Then he said, "Your team reminds me of the teams I had the most fun coaching. Nothing fancy. Great running back. You play hard. Boy, your kids play hard. You don't hot dog. Now, of course, I hope you stumble today. But you guys have my kind of team."

In the tunnel just prior to the start of the game we experienced one of the greatest emotional surges I've ever been through. It was a special moment for our coaches: Our players were so wired, so electrified, we had to try to settle them down. They were making so much noise and we still had to wait another minute for TV before we went out. I kept saying, "Settle down, settle down," but at that point, I couldn't say a lot to get control. I let go.

We wanted to make an immediate statement, so when we won the coin toss we took the ball instead of deferring possession to the second half. We drove 73 yards on 12 plays to open the game, with Darnell scoring the first of his three touchdowns. We never looked back.

We won 21–10 and it was a mob scene on the field when I went to do a TV interview with Lynn Swann. On the way off the field I asked the police escorts to stop for a minute. I got up on the bench on the Penn State side of the field and absorbed the bedlam for 15 or 20 seconds. I wanted to soak in it.

This scene, this energy, was something that in my wildest dreams I could imagine, but I couldn't know it was really achievable until it actually happened. Now it was right there in front of me. It was simply overwhelming.

When I began my postgame press conference, I made a face of mock shock and said, "We must be pretty good."

18.

Fairy Dust

*"Trust is the basic ingredient of all organizations,
the lubrication that maintains the organization, and it
is as mysterious and elusive a concept as leadership—
and as important.... If trust is to be generated, there must
be predictability: The capacity to predict another's behavior.
The ability to predict outcomes with a high probability
of success generates and maintains trust."*
—Dennis Kroner

In my office I keep a blown-up picture of a 1963 *Sports Illustrated* cover featuring Northwestern's line. I'm going to replace it, though, with the cover of the November 1995 issue featuring Darnell.

It was not necessarily our goal to be on the *SI* cover, but it does have a certain aura and credibility attached to it. I think we were supposed to be on the cover after the Notre Dame game, but I believe that was the week Cal Ripken broke Lou Gehrig's record. Now that we had gotten that distinction, though, of course we worried about the hex or jinx that supposedly comes with the territory.

Actually, we had more on our mind. We were going up against Iowa, the team that had embarrassed us ever since I'd been here. Hayden's words in 1992—about hoping they hadn't hurt any of our boys—still were fresh to me.

The Hawkeyes had beaten us 21 times in a row now but they had lost their last three games entering our game. I figured they'd play with the nasty, desperate temperament of a wounded animal. We poured salt in those wounds that week, too, when Rob Johnson committed what I consider the only media mistake we made all season.

I had made a statement that we had been waiting for this game all year and that we had admired Iowa because of its ability to punish us over the years. When Rob was asked to comment on that he said, "Not only are we going to win, we're going to hurt them."

It was just not smart on Rob's part. Before the Notre Dame game he had gotten away with telling the media to "tell Coach Holtz to watch out." Somehow that just went by the wayside. This didn't, and the war of words escalated rapidly.

Everybody was trying to get us to say something. A few of the kids in Iowa responded to Rob's comment, and Hayden Fry said some things that were unlike him. He denied that he'd ever run up the score against us although we all know he did in 1992. Then he challenged the validity of our accomplishments.

"Across America in sports," he said, "you're going to have teams jump up and do well from time to time. But that's not the barometer to judge. You need to do it over the long haul and see how long you're really competitive."

I think part of this hostility stems from the fact that I don't think Iowa and Hayden really understand where we were coming from in red-lettering the game. It really was as sincere a compliment as we could give them, but I think they took it as an insult. Our guys really have gotten into the rivalry over the years. Now, after we give our scout team the Iowa helmet decals for the week, we make them stretch at the other end of the field. They become the enemy.

That's all in fun, or so we thought. Now it was developing into a real grudge game, which wasn't what I had in mind. We were in a real flow, really businesslike, and I didn't want us to be in a situation where we were too emotional and tense and making foolish mistakes.

On film Iowa had been very physical against Michigan State and exactly the opposite against Illinois. We didn't know which team we were going to get. If we got the team that played Michigan State, we knew we'd have our hands full. If we got the one that played Illinois, well, we were going to win.

It was a miserable day for football, about 20 degrees, windy, and snowing—and we still had our third straight home sellout.

Iowa came out absolutely smoking. It was, in fact, the team that had played Michigan State. They were big, they were strong, and they were good, and they held us to 188 yards in total offense.

All season, though, we had concocted ways to win. This time Brian Musso ran a punt back 60 yards for a spectacular touchdown and Hudhaifa Ismaeli scored on a fumble return late in the fourth quarter. Those plays accounted for the margin of victory: We won 31–20, but it didn't feel like 31–20. Iowa controlled the game all the way.

They extracted a severe price for their loss, though: Pat Fitzgerald had broken his leg, would need surgery, and be out for the season. As terrific as it was to shed a 21-year burden, this was a sobering footnote. Fitz had become an incredible player and was part of the soul of our team. Even Hayden Fry recognized that and I appreciate that he wrote Fitz the next week.

Our defense had been winning games for us all year and our statistics were almost absurd. Throughout the regular season we gave up 12.7 points a game—a year after giving up 32 a game. No team in the nation gave up fewer points than we did and our turnover ratio was among the very best.

We didn't beat ourselves, and that's a great starting point. That way, you only have to beat one team. The problems start when you have to play against two.

Without Fitz, though, everybody was going to have to pick it up. You don't lose the Big Ten defensive player of the year without being affected by it. But we emphasized that we weren't a one-man team and that this just meant a chance for somebody else to contribute.

I visited Fitz in the hospital the day after the game, and they already had put two screws in his ankle. All he could talk about was how eager he was to get out and start helping Donnie Holmes take his place.

We were 9–1 now but Ohio State beat Illinois that week and remained undefeated. The way we looked at it, however, one game still stood in the way of us being at least Big Ten co-champions. So we didn't talk about Ohio State, or the Ohio State–Michigan game, or any of that.

All we knew was that if we beat Purdue we were entitled to rings and a trophy. On Tuesday I told the seniors we were going to start designing the ring. I wanted to put them even further into a position of accountability. Ordinarily I wouldn't do something like that, and some of my coaches told me it was a mistake. But my hunch was it was the right time to do it.

To give the guys a visual idea of the significance of a championship, I had all the coaches bring in their championship rings and bowl watches. We had quite a number, and we put them on display before the kids walked into the Thursday meeting.

This was a magnificent opportunity and we weren't going to

slack off now. The payoff for our discipline, our hard work, was being reaped. The lessons of getting in the wheelbarrow and priming the pump were coming to life. And we really did live the value of faith.

Purdue was 3-5-1 but was probably the best 3-5-1 team you've ever seen. Early in the year the Boilermakers could easily have won games against Notre Dame, Michigan, Michigan State, and Penn State and changed the complexion of their season.

But even if Purdue had been playing with the confidence of having won a few more, I'm not sure what could have slowed us down at that point. At our breakfast Thursday, I again asked the seniors what they needed from the coaches. This time they looked me in the eye and said, "Coach, just get us to the game on time."

They didn't say it in a cocky way. They said it like "Let us take care of this one. There isn't anybody or anything that can keep it from us." Again, I tried to just step aside. The water was gushing out of the pump.

That was how the game went, too. Everything seemed to flow, and we always were pretty well in control. We had a couple of big plays in the first half—Chris Martin returned an interception 76 yards for a touchdown and Steve Schnur hit D'Wayne Bates on a 72-yard touchdown pass. In the first two minutes of the second half we went ahead 23–0 on a safety and a quarterback sneak.

We won 23–8—now we were at least co-champions. I told the media, "The glass slipper's broken. Cinderella threw it against the wall and smashed it to pieces." But what I'll take most from that day probably has less to do with the victory than with the way we went about it. We had conducted ourselves well all season, but this special day served to really illuminate that for me.

First of all, the game was so cleanly played on both sides. None of our guys showboated or hotdogged. When Purdue's Mike Alstott broke the school's career rushing record, the game was stopped to honor him and he ran to the opposite end of the field to give the ball to his parents. Our guys heartily congratulated him, too.

On Chris Martin's interception, Casey Dailey hit their quarterback, picked the kid up afterward and patted him on the butt. Replays of that were shown over and over on national television and it captured what our team was about. People thought of us and remembered us that way. We won humbly and honorably.

Our kids would score and hand the ball right to the official in the end zone. They were eloquent in their interviews. They were tremendous sportsmen, and even the Purdue players noted it.

"I wish they were really bad sports because I really wanted to hate them," Purdue defensive tackle Jayme Washel told reporters after the game. "They're the best team in the Big Ten. Ohio State has the best athletes but they're the best team."

To me, that was as great a compliment as being called relentless. Everybody hopes that athletes will play with class but it seems to have dwindled in importance. We seem to have come to a point where we more readily accept poor behavior; perhaps it is a byproduct of the tremendous exposure the pros' antics and high salaries receive. Somehow, it has become okay for sportsmanship and humility to go by the wayside if you're tremendously talented.

When I picture how I would want an ideal season to look, I see us winning with grace and dignity. It should be the norm, but unfortunately it's the exception. You shouldn't have to feel so proud of the exception, I guess, but I sure was.

We had "Big Ten Championship" hats and shirts waiting for the kids on the sideline, and when our players got them, they ran right over to the 5,000 or so fans of ours who had come to West Lafayette. The players could only get so far, though, because the fans had swept onto the field toward them. It was jubilation city.

Jim Delany, the commissioner of the Big Ten, came into our locker room to present the championship trophy. I sat back and took a mental picture I'll keep from the season: I looked at the guys beaming as they accepted the trophy, and it was one of the most fulfilling sensations I've ever had.

The vision we had, the top of our jigsaw puzzle, was nearly complete. To see these guys who had been ridiculed and abused for so long, man, did they deserve this moment.

In the Nicolet Center, we had painted on the wall the years Northwestern had won championship—and "1-9-9-?" We went back and painted in "5." And then we waited. And waited. And waited.

We were ranked fourth now but our regular season was over and Ohio State still was undefeated and ranked second. If the Buckeyes beat 18th-ranked Michigan later in the week, they were going to the Rose Bowl and we were going to the Citrus Bowl. If they lost or were tied, we'd go to the Rose Bowl.

If I got asked once, I got asked a hundred times: Who did I think would win? And I'd say, "I think Michigan will win. I think

Michigan is the best team we've played all year." I meant that, but I also repeatedly said that Ohio State was a terrific team and that if it won, it deserved to represent our conference.

But I also was counting on there being a little fairy dust around for our benefit.

Some people tried to make a big deal out of what I'd said, like I'd shown Ohio State disrespect. Those who suggested that mis-construed me. Besides, didn't it make sense that we would root for Michigan in this case?

Even if what I had said was going to be used against us, I think Terry Glenn of Ohio State made up for it when he said, "Michigan is nobody. I guarantee we're going to the Rose Bowl."

We had so many media requests that week that I didn't really have time to stew over the situation. We had to get busy putting to-gether our bowl itineraries, for either scenario, so there were a million logistical things to contend with.

The week also offered a nice respite. On Thanksgiving Day Mary and I had a contest: She cooked a turkey in the oven, and I cooked one outside on the grill. I think the turkey she got me to cook was 28 pounds, so the contest basically was fixed. I burnt mine to a crisp. On Friday, we went to watch Clay play in the city of Chicago championship football game.

Game day came at last—even if it wasn't exactly what I think of as game day. It was strange to have so much depending on some-thing we could only watch. We had a party at Nicolet and ABC, ESPN and probably six or seven other television crews were there to keep an eye on us. Most of the game the media outnumbered us because many of the guys had gone home for Thanksgiving and some had gone over to Ann Arbor. As the game progressed fans and people from all over campus started migrating to Nico-let. The outer rooms were crammed.

I kept pretty quiet during the game, partly because about 10 minutes into it I became conscious of the fact that every funny look or sound I made would be on television. I almost felt I would have to find a place to hide if I got emotional, because I didn't want to be obnoxious.

From the opening play, though, when Tim Biakabutuka ran 22 yards, I just knew Michigan was going to win. From there I sort of leaned back and watched everything unfold—as if I could do anything else. One of the newspapers reported that I got itchy with Michigan leading late in the game and said, "Show the clock!" When it said "3:46," I said, "Holy Smokes."

Michigan won 31–23, and Biakabutuka finished with 313 yards. I'd still have to look up Touchdown Tim's last name to spell it, but when I was asked later if I knew how, I said: "T-I-M-T-D-T-H-A-N-K-Y-O-U."

After the game I was especially thankful, happy, and relieved for Larry Curry. Miami of Ohio undeniably was a team loss for us, as any loss would be, but I was worried Larry would forever take that on his shoulders if that game kept us from the Rose Bowl.

Now Larry could shrug that off and always be known for what he should be known: as a vital part of our Rose Bowl team.

19.

Temptation

"Everybody asked me last season why we won, and I say, 'Coach Barnett.' Then they say, 'Is that all? Is that all?' And I say, 'Yeah—that's all.' He's very charismatic, and he's always been honest. And, I don't know what it is exactly, but you just kind of believe in the guy."
—Pat Fitzgerald

In the month leading up to the Rose Bowl we faced a different kind of chaos. The attention on us increased geometrically. So did the focus on me.

I was courted by other schools and I wasn't always sure how to deal with it. I believe my general approach, though, was sound: I wouldn't close any doors and I would listen to anything—but ultimately any decision would be based on what was best for my family.

Some people took issue with my willingness to consider other job possibilities, but that's part of the nature of the business. In coaching, there's a very small time window where a job may be open.

On the way back from the Michigan game vice president Bill Fischer had said that Northwestern wanted to have a discussion about extending my contract. I was in the fourth year of my original five-year contract. (I did receive an extension in 1994, but I had some leeway). In early November I talked over what I would need and what I thought would be fair with my close friend, Mizzou classmate, and lawyer, Rocky Walther.

That's right, a lawyer: I thought it was a good idea to have one after I "negotiated" my first Northwestern contract.

My priorities could be broken into thirds:

First, commitments to getting things done so Northwestern

could be at least close to even with other programs in the Big Ten. I mean, I didn't want anybody lobbing pitches to us, but I at least wanted to be swinging with the same-size bat as everybody else. We still were not on a level playing field in, well, you name the category.

Our equipment budget was $50,000 below anybody else's in the conference. Our recruiting budget was $80,000 below the second-lowest in the conference. We're allowed to pay for summer school for 20 students; the Big Ten average is 55.

We needed another strength coach. We were way behind in our allocation there, and our guys were tremendously overworked. We needed another secretary. We needed more audio-visual help.

I think it's worth noting that we didn't request anything that had to do with lowering academic standards for our recruits. To me, that was one of the parameters I understood when I came in. That was the essence of the university.

I did ask for help with our walk-on program: As it was, if you hadn't applied for admission here by January 1 you couldn't come to school the next fall. All I wanted was the flexibility to be able to bring in for admission consideration somebody who hadn't gotten a scholarship anywhere by the time the February signing period passed.

It's really hard for us to get walk-ons, anyway, because school is so expensive. But with schools now limited to 85 scholarships for football, it's critical to have quality walk-ons.

My second priority was certain assurances for my staff. I asked for cost-of-living raises, bowl bonuses, and retention bonuses for staying a certain number of years. My third priority was my salary and personal interests.

We submitted the list sometime in November and by the time we had earned the Rose Bowl bid I still hadn't heard back from Northwestern. I was under the impression we would have heard something by then but I didn't have anything in my hands and didn't know what Northwestern was going to offer me.

Some people indirectly affiliated with Georgia called shortly after we had earned the Rose Bowl bid. And as I was checking into my hotel in Pasadena for a preliminary Rose Bowl press conference, a UCLA representative called. Terry Donahue, the UCLA coach, had called a few days earlier and said he was thinking about retiring and wondered if I would consider the job. I told the UCLA rep the same things I told Terry and would say all along:

I didn't know what kind of offer Northwestern was going to come back with. Yes, it would probably be in my best interest to listen to what UCLA had to say but ... let's just see what happens. Right now I'm more concerned about this bowl game than anything else.

Still, never in my wildest dreams did I ever think I would have the opportunity to be the coach at Georgia or UCLA—and a few other prestigious places, as it turned out. I don't dream about those kinds of things, actually, so I guess a better way to say it is I would never have predicted I'd have such opportunities.

The morning of the press conference in Pasadena I told Rick Taylor I'd been contacted by representatives of Georgia and UCLA. I told him I told Georgia I'd meet with them but I wasn't sure yet about UCLA. He said he wasn't surprised I'd heard from them, then said, "I can't see you at Georgia," and told me he would get on Northwestern to expedite its proposal.

I called Vince Dooley, the Georgia athletic director. He was eager to get their situation resolved and he flew to Chicago the night of my return from the press conference to meet me at O'Hare. I met with Vince for about two hours and he explained the arrangements and salary and those types of things. When I left that meeting, my interest was tweaked considerably.

With recruiting—which you can never let up on—and bowl preparation and accepting some of the awards that were coming in, my upcoming schedule was going to be hectic. So I told Mary, "Why don't you fly down to Georgia and take a look and get a read on it? I need to know how you feel about this, and if you don't want to live there it makes no sense for me to carry this out any further. It wouldn't even make any sense for me to go look."

Mary felt fine about the idea, and Vince went for it, too. The next day, Vince's wife, Barbara, called and they arranged for Mary to go down a few days later. We had a recruiting weekend in between—recruiting was going great—and Georgia really was not on my mind. Nor was UCLA. Our players were jacked up about Pasadena, and I was basking in their excitement.

On Sunday, I left for a five- or six-day trip through places like San Antonio, Orlando, and Tampa. I needed to recruit and had agreed to do a few TV tapings. Northwestern hadn't come up with a new contract by the time I left, but I wasn't losing time worrying about it. Mary left for Athens, Georgia, on Monday.

Although Mary and I thought she could travel incognito, it

didn't work out that way. When she landed in Atlanta, standing at the gate where she got off the plane was Mark McCairens—the president of the Northwestern booster club. He said, "Mary, what are you doing here?" Mary couldn't lie, and when she told him his jaw just dropped. That was a little awkward for her.

When I spoke with Mary on the phone late Monday night and asked what she thought of Georgia, she said, "Well, you know, it's kind of nice. The people are so nice. I could like it here."

The next few days were a whirlwind. I was in Orlando recruiting and taping a show at Disney World late in the week. The Heisman Trophy was going to be announced on Saturday and Darnell Autry had been invited to the ceremony.

When I was at Colorado and Darian Hagan was in the voting, Mac offered me the chance to go to the ceremony because I was Darian's position coach. I thought that was special, so I had offered John Wristen the same opportunity with Darnell and John really wanted to do it. So I had already planned to send John instead of me; I also knew I was going to be on the road at that time. I guess I say all this because I got a lot of letters and phone calls from people wondering why I wasn't in New York, and I want it known that I hadn't snubbed Darnell.

As I looked at the schedule from Orlando, and looked at the fact that Northwestern still hadn't sent its proposal, I thought it might be a convenient time for me to stop in Athens. I'd never been to the campus. I thought, what the heck—I can fly to Atlanta, drive over and spend an hour or two in Athens and go back to Chicago that night. I called Vince, and he thought it was a great idea.

I really liked what I saw at Georgia. It was absolutely a first-class operation, just about ideal. The A.D. was the former football coach and the team had every resource. The football stadium was the most beautiful I'd ever been in.

The only small concern I had was that Vince thought I should keep a few members of the former staff for transition purposes, and I didn't think that was necessarily a good idea. I wanted to bring in all my own people.

I thought we had pulled this visit off quietly and subtly until the outgoing coach, Ray Goff, caught sight of me. When I called in to the office for messages that afternoon there already were a couple from TV stations in Athens. When the papers called my response—and it was accurate—was, "I was in the area and

180

thought I would stop by and see it, because I had never been there."

Then I got a phone call from someone representing another university, which I'm not going to name, but the opportunity was considerable. I was confused enough as it was and I didn't want to be thinking about those things at the time, anyway, so I declined to follow up.

Now it was a week or so into December and I still hadn't heard anything from Northwestern. They would probably tell you that they didn't know they were supposed to be in a hurry but my understanding had been otherwise. But I think once some of this stuff got in the papers, their sense of urgency picked up.

On December 10 Northwestern faxed Rocky and me their contract proposal. It was pretty good for the program and for the assistants and somewhat less than what we had hoped for me personally. I was prepared not to get everything I asked for, so I thought what they had done was pretty fair. Probably a year before, I would have thought it was really fair.

But it was hard not to compare the offer with what Georgia and the other schools were talking about. I mean, it was easily the lowest of the three offers, and UCLA's still was to come. We let Northwestern know it was third out of three, and at that time some of the trustees let me know they thought I'd been out of line going to Georgia. I also had gotten a few notes condemning me for visiting there.

But, you know, I didn't think I was out of line. I told them I had no idea what my worth was on the market, and I wasn't out trying to find out what it was. But I'd had three schools where I hadn't coached a day offer me a lot of money, and my own university, where we just produced a Big Ten championship for the first time since 1936, was third in the running. They said, "We're Northwestern, not Georgia. Surely you didn't expect us to keep up with those other two schools?"

I said, "Well, yeah, I sort of did."

We adjourned, and I didn't know what to make of this and how to take what they were saying. Rocky and I went back to my house. Mary said she could feel the whole thing getting nasty, and she wondered whether this issue was going to dominate the next few weeks.

She suggested calling everybody and putting everything on hold until after the Rose Bowl. I agreed. I wanted to see our players in the Rose Bowl and that was it. I didn't want to be distracted and I didn't want to become a distraction myself.

Vince Dooley was out of town when I called so I left him a message that I was very interested but wasn't going to make any decisions until after the game. If he had to hire somebody before then, I understood. At one point he had told me they might be willing to wait until after the bowl. I didn't know how he felt now but I figured if he was able to wait, it might work out, and if he wasn't, then that's the way it was supposed to be and I wasn't meant to go.

I let Northwestern know that I was going to wait to decide but I told them that we could resolve it if they were willing to come up with such-and-such and such-and-such, which still was going to be dramatically less than the minimum I would get at the other places. Well, Northwestern came up with some alternatives, but there was still a gulf and I became exasperated by the spirit of the negotiations.

At about this time I expressed my concerns with a friend who works in our business school, Kellogg. He offered perspective and advice I hadn't considered. He said, "You need to understand that no one here has ever gone through this situation before. They don't understand the market." Then he said, "Can you forgive them?"

Those last words made a serious impact. Could I forgive them? Once I resolved to myself that, yes, I could, my unrest eased up. I felt empowered. I must admit, however, that I would have to visualize and remind myself of that statement a number of times in the months of negotiations before we came to a final agreement in May.

I had asked our kids not to pay attention to the negotiations so I had to be the same way. I had to be exemplary or they were going to become victims of the situation. I realized that this was all a real reach for Northwestern and, since I had never made much, I wasn't as hung up on the money as I was on the fairness of the deal.

Vince called and said he would have to proceed with another coach, but I still greatly appreciate how Georgia treated me. They ended up hiring Jim Donnan from Marshall after Kansas' Glen Mason accepted the job but then changed his mind.

Soon afterward, Terry Donahue did resign at UCLA, and that commenced a new swirl of rumors. I got a few calls from various representatives of UCLA wanting to at least talk to me, but I said I'd have to let them know later.

* * *

Meanwhile, our practices were going exceptionally well, and my role by now had become more facilitator than anything else. These guys were on automatic.

During this time I was so impressed by the way the university was handling all the Rose Bowl logistics and publicity matters. Initially, the university seemed more worried about saving money than doing it right, but, fortunately, a decision was made to approach it all in a first-class manner. And that's how it went, from the first day to the last. I salute our president, Henry Bienen, and Rick Taylor for what they got done.

We were undermanned, understaffed, and under-resourced, but somehow we got it done. The people in sports information, Brad Hurlbut, Lisa Juscik, and Mark Simpson, were particularly unbelievable; they did the work that staffs twice as large do—and without even having the benefit of a secretary. I also was amazed by the accomplishments of Jack Freeman, our assistant athletic director in charge of facilities.

The phone calls never slowed down in December and, as flattering as it was, I think it began to take a toll on us. It wasn't unusual for our assistants to have 10 or 15 messages a day, and some days there were around 100 calls for me. One day I received 40 requests for speaking engagements.

Still, I think we mostly maintained our focus and drowned out the hype. An outsider might look at it differently, but I had been in two Orange Bowls for national championships and I'm certain that this group was better tuned in than either of those teams.

We arrived in California on December 17 and set up in Newport Beach. We'd practice during the day, and at night the staff would go out recruiting: San Diego, Los Angeles, Seattle. The team took trips to Universal Studios and Disneyland, and appeared on the *Tonight Show*.

We didn't impose a curfew on the team during the trip, and you might be able to understand why from the compliments our guys were getting. On the plane out the flight attendant said she couldn't believe this was a football team because of how considerate and respectful they were. When we checked out of our Newport Beach hotel to move over to Pasadena, the manager said in his 20 years there this was the classiest group of kids he'd ever been around. One of the guys unloading trucks in Pasadena said the same thing.

We closed our practices in California but not because we were getting uptight or engaging in some cloak-and-dagger deal. It was mostly because it was the only time we could have any privacy and let loose and yell and really have a good time. It was nourishing.

UCLA called again during this time and I agreed to meet with them since they were right in the neighborhood—but with the provision that our talk was purely informational and I would not be making any decisions until after the game. It was a fact-finding mission. Mostly, it was them explaining their expectations and me explaining my misgivings about living in L.A.

Around the 27th we were getting very anxious to play this sucker. That's about when I got a call from somebody representing Oklahoma. Actually, they talked to me through Rocky, and Rocky told them I'd be interested in listening but couldn't meet with them until after the game.

Oklahoma didn't want to wait and they hired John Blake a day or two later. UCLA, though, called again and wanted me to meet with the chancellor, Charles Young, and the A.D., Pete Dalis.

We had the morning of the 31st clear, so I agreed to meet with them down at Disney studios. As the discussion went on, I could sense Dr. Young really wanting me to take the job. Everything they said was terrific, everything they did was terrific, and they seemed willing to go any extra distance in order to make it happen.

I told them that Rocky was coming in later that day and that we should all talk immediately after the Rose Bowl.

20.

The Wall of Jericho

"And seven priests shall bear before the
ark seven trumpets of rams' horns: and the seventh
day ye shall compass the city seven times, and
the priests shall blow with the trumpets.... And when
ye hear the sound of the trumpet, all the
people shall shout with a great shout; and the
wall of the city shall fall down flat ..."
—The Book of Joshua, 6:4-5

The first time the kids walked into the Rose Bowl was at noon on December 31. It was the first time they could see its magnificent setting, surrounded by the San Gabriel Mountains, the first time they could see that purple painted in the end zone. They were dazzled.

We stayed in downtown L.A. to keep away from the hubbub. I called Steve Musseau that night—he lives in Idaho, but we had invited him to be our guest—and we talked about a disappointing development.

A petty mind at some other school had read of Steve's involvement in our program and reported to the NCAA that Steve was an extra coach. This was brought to the attention of our administration, who told me that during the game Steve could not stand within the area of the players' box and could not speak with our players.

To me, it was incredible that the NCAA would bother dictating this—and even more incredible that another school would make an issue of it. This guy doesn't coach. This guy is like the team's grandfather.

Steve was a little upset and angered but he still wanted to deliver a message to the team at our practice the day before the game. His talk had to do with the wall of Jericho and Joshua, who marched around the city seven times before the wall fell. Steve's

185

message was that we were at Jericho. When he finished he handed me a key and said, "Joshua, here's your key."

I had decided long before that there was only one thing I wanted to do to celebrate making it to the Rose Bowl, and I wanted it to be private. All I wanted was to go to the Rose Bowl by myself the night before the game, walk onto the field ... and jump as high as I could.

That was all I really wanted out of the entire trip. I don't think I'd ever stopped to take it in or indulge myself in any appreciation of what had happened. But I was always counting on having this precious moment. The only thing I had in mind was wanting to be in there and feel my heart beat against my chest and just grab on to a small sense of accomplishment. It was so fulfilling to have delivered on the promise: taking the Purple to Pasadena.

That's probably all you need in life—to be able to fulfill your promises.

So I made arrangements to go out there at 10 o'clock that night. It was so windy that there were concerns that some of the Rose Bowl floats might get blown over. Inside the stadium, though, it was really calm.

When I arrived at the Bowl there were a few security guards inside. They turned the stadium lights on for me, and there was dew on the grass. It was an amazing sight. When I reached the field, the only two people I could see were two guards, one at each end of the field, each wrapped in blankets and just watching me.

As I began walking toward the field, I swear, I lost control of my body and just kept going around the perimeter. Once I started I couldn't stop. I walked around seven times and then I leaped as high as I could, which wasn't very high.

Then I turned around, walked off the field, got back in the car and went back to the hotel.

In chapel the next morning, Larry Lilja talked about the notion of being programmed to win.

His example came from the movie *The Terminator*, where Arnold Schwarzenegger plays a cyborg who relentlessly chases the person he was programmed to kill. Even when the cyborg had only its head and arm left, it continued the chase. I believe Larry avoided the word "kill" but it still made for an interesting chapel session.

New Year's Day was a splendid day for football and I'll never forget the sight of coming down into the valley where the Rose

Bowl is and seeing the massive parking lot completely full. Getting dressed wasn't much different than for any other game but when we went out on the field to warm up we entered a world unlike any we had ever seen.

Out of the 55,000 or so Northwestern fans (in the 100,000-seat stadium), 99% of them must have been wearing purple. It was almost mystical. It was the stuff movies and dreams are made of.

USC had been to 27 Rose Bowls in the time we'd been to one but that wasn't what worried us going into the game.

It was going to be hard to get used to the speed of the game after such a long layoff, and it was going to be particularly hard against a team with the extreme speed of the Trojans. I also thought it would be crucial to minimize their third-down conversions. That probably was the only area all season we had been weak in defending and they were the best in the Pacific 10 in that category.

What I didn't expect was for us to lose the turnover battle—we played against ourselves for the first time all season—and for them to come out throwing ... and throwing. I think we adjusted reasonably well to the no-huddle offense they used but we really never made them run the ball. They threw 39 times but it seemed like 90.

They went 83 yards on their first drive and it immediately became clear we were going to have fits containing Keyshawn Johnson, their wide receiver. Even when we knew they were going to throw to him we couldn't prevent it. He parted the seas like you-know-who. He ended up with 12 catches, all for first downs, and set a Rose Bowl-record with 216 receiving yards.

Their quarterback, Brad Otton, was awesome. He had the game of a lifetime: He was finding the third receiver option, and we would hit him and just bounce off while he was throwing. I didn't think Otton would be able to keep that up all game.

We got our bearings after their first score and tied it with Darnell's three-yard run. But then USC asserted itself with the next 17 points. I do have questions about the last seven of those.

Trailing 17–7 we were gaining large chunks of territory when Schnur threw to Brian Musso who wheeled upfield and was near the 50-yard line when his knee hit the ground and he lost the ball. USC's Daylon McCutcheon scooped it up and ran 53 yards for a touchdown.

I referred to the play as a "quote, unquote, fumble" after the game. It took me almost three months before I watched the

187

game again and I can't say I could tell from the film whether it was a fumble or not. At the time it seemed quite clear that it wasn't.

Either way, though, the ruling is what matters. It was just too bad because I really think we were on our way to scoring and that play caused a 14-point swing and gave them a 24–7 lead. We were able to salvage something and slow their momentum late in the half when Tim Scharf stripped the ball from a USC runner and Brian Gowins kicked a 29-yard field goal with two seconds left.

Because of that, and the realization of how quickly 14 points swung on the fumble runback, I think we were calm at halftime despite being down 24–10. We didn't feel we had lost our grip on the game, and I reminded them of the *Terminator* theme.

"Men," I said, "all we've got left now is a head and an arm, but we are programmed to win this game. They cannot stop us. We are not dead." Then I told them we were going to go score and then recover an onside kick and score again.

We had spent time working on our onside kick and we considered opening the game with one. But there was no guarantee it would work out and I thought it would be better for us to get the feeling of running down the field and getting the energy flowing with some hitting.

Hudhaifa returned the second-half kickoff to our 43-yard line, and now we knew the momentum was with us. We went right down and made a field goal and then Brian kicked the perfect onside kick. We caught them completely by surprise, and Josh Barnes recovered it at midfield. Six plays later, Darnell scored and now it was 24–19.

According to the chart we use to assess whether or not to go for a two-point conversion, this was a situation where we should go for it. A successful conversion would put us in position to tie with a field goal. And, really, I reacted automatically because I didn't give any thought to how many more scores there might be.

The chart is predicated on the other team not scoring again and, as a coach, it's hard to ever concede that the other team will score again. Maybe I had a false sense of security, and maybe I should have asked Vandy if he thought we were ready to contain them.

Maybe next time I'm in that situation I'll try to account for that. But in retrospect, hey, I liked our two-point plan and thought it would work. But Schnur's pass went incomplete, and that hurt later.

USC scored next but then we roared back with two touchdowns to go ahead 32–31 early in the fourth quarter. When that happened, the crowd noise was like a thunder clap. We had scored on five possessions in a row and I believed there was no way we were going to give up the lead. I mean, we had already given up more points than we had in any game all season.

According to script we went for two here again. Again, it did not work out, but this one I have no doubt we should have attempted because it would have been ridiculous at that stage to give them a chance to win the game with a field goal.

USC kicked a field goal on its next drive to go ahead 34–32 but we immediately got moving again on our next series. We were in Trojan territory when a pass just got away from Schnur. He played sensationally, and it was probably the only poor ball he threw all day—and one of the few all season. USC's Jesse Davis picked it off and they drove to go ahead 41–32 with 2:52 left.

After all it had taken to get here, we weren't going to let go while we still had a breath. We weren't going to let go even if the Terminator only had an arm now.

We drove down the field and D'Wayne made a great catch in the end zone—only for it to be called back because of a holding penalty. It got to be fourth and long with 41 seconds remaining, and we called timeout to assess our chances of making the first down.

Brian Gowins said, "Coach, you know, we're going to need a field goal, anyway, so why don't we do it now? There's no wind, and a 49-yarder is within my reach." I listened to Brian and I thought the reasoning was good: We would need to score twice, and our chances of kicking a 49-yard field goal seemed greater than converting a fourth-and-10 pass.

Brian had had a funny week of practice in Newport Beach and Pasadena. I mean, he must have hit the uprights 10 or 11 times and I had joked with him about it a few times:

"Man, you are good," I would tell him. "There are a lot of guys who can't hit the upright to save their life. Most guys try to kick it between the two, but you're not settling for that. You're narrowing it down to one spot. That is accuracy!"

So when Brian's kick hit the left upright and bounced off no good, that's why I smiled the smile I did. A lot of people have written me and commented about that. I looked skyward and just thought ... Man, we gave it a heck of a shot.

There were a lot of tears in the locker room after the game and I wished I had the words to console the guys and make them still feel as good about themselves as they should have. In the immediate aftermath of defeat, though, I didn't expect to be able to soothe them. Or myself.

But I made sure I let them know that the game itself, as much as it weighed on us at the moment, would not define our season or cast a shadow over it. I told them we would hang on to the beauty and rewards of this season for the rest of our lives.

We'd emerged from such adversity the last three years—the last 47 years, really—and there was no way this loss would put a blemish on that. I told them, though, that our approach now had to be that we need to come back to the Rose Bowl ... and win it.

21.

The Difference

*"And there is a Catskill eagle in some souls
that can alike dive down into the blackest gorges and
soar out of them and become invisible in the sunny
spaces, and even if he forever flies within the gorge, that
gorge is in the mountains, so that even in his lowest
swoop the mountain eagle is still higher than the birds
upon the plains even though they soar."*
—Herman Melville

About two weeks before the Rose Bowl I had reluctantly agreed to do a *Nightline* interview after the game. President Bienen had asked me to do it but I didn't want to because I thought it was risky. I don't think people quite understand the emotions you go through in a game, especially when you lose it. I should have said no.

We did the interview from Pasadena about two hours after the game and waiting around there was the last thing I wanted to do at the time. Forrest Sawyer did the interview, and I would describe it as an "in-your-face" job. It was not fun, and I really felt Sawyer had put me on the spot at a hard time.

After the *Nightline* episode we all went back to my suite in the hotel. The group included my mom, Mary, Courtney and Clay, and close friends. People breezed in and out for a few hours.

We began discussing the game, and then the talk turned to UCLA. For the first time, I was really assessing the job. The only new information I'd picked up in the last few days was that I had thoroughly enjoyed the L.A. weather. Believe me, as we sat there on the balcony in the comfortable 70 degrees and overlooked the lights, there seemed to be a lot of positives.

Mary, the kids, and I had gone for a drive one Sunday while we were out there. We went by O.J.'s house, went over to Pacific

Palisades, went up around Sunset Boulevard and by the Bel-Air Country Club.

It was all pretty nice but Mary and Lisa Vanderlinden had taken a peek at the housing situation and it looked like all the assistants would have to live at least 45 minutes away. Because of that Mary was not excited about UCLA. She would have gone, but she loved Chicago and had pain in her heart about the idea of the staff living so far away.

Mary and I went around the balcony and asked everybody what we should do. Clay was all for UCLA; he was ready to go. Courtney was really concerned about what kind of hits she'd take at Northwestern if I left, and I was worried about that, too.

Even though Rick Taylor had described my proposed Northwestern contract as "L&L"—long and lots—some aspects of it still weren't meeting my expectations. And now, with the bowl finished, I allowed myself to really feel frustration with Northwestern. I wanted it to be resolved and over with, and to stay at Northwestern, but I felt like they just weren't allowing it to happen.

I felt real resentment about having to scratch and claw and beg for things about which four other schools had said, "Well, yeah, that's the way it's supposed to be." At Georgia and UCLA, for instance, they knew what it was going to take to win and were willing to provide it. Period.

The resentment would build to a certain point and I'd hear the little voice saying, "Can you forgive them?" So I would, but then my resentment would float back up.

The morning after the game Rocky went down to meet with UCLA to discuss the specifics of their offer. By now the papers were going crazy with this, and I had refused to comment. Somebody wrote that by doing so I hadn't taken advantage of the opportunity to set everything straight. Maybe, but how could I set something straight that wasn't straight?

We met as a staff while Rocky was at UCLA and I told them we had been offered the job at UCLA and I was really thinking hard about it. At that moment, in fact, I probably was UCLA-bound. I asked each of my coaches where they stood on it. There were two guys who were ready to go. Everybody else I was uncertain about.

We returned from Pasadena to Chicago that Tuesday. I had to leave for North Carolina the next morning on a recruiting trip but I told my staff to talk it over with their families and we'd hash

192

it out on Wednesday. Rocky told me about his discussion with UCLA and he kept saying, "These people are so great to work with." Northwestern's offer now was fifth out of five.

I told UCLA I'd answer them Thursday.

On Tuesday's flight back to Chicago I talked to Sam Valenzisi and asked him if all this speculation on my future was disrupting the players.

"No, not really," he said. "Right now, though, everybody expects you're going to move on." When I asked him why, he said, "Well, it's California, and you like golf and you like warm weather." In his own sarcastic way he added, "So I guess I won't be seeing much of you anymore?" That's Sam.

But he sure wasn't the only one thinking that way. The Northwestern administration apparently was convinced that I was leaving and even approached Ron Vanderlinden about taking over if I left—which is exactly what the administration should have done.

When we arrived at O'Hare on Tuesday the media were all over the place and it seemed like not one of the reporters wanted to talk to the players. They all came right for me. I was upset that my negotiations had become such a big story. I did not want it to get to that, especially to the exclusion of the team.

The recruit I went to see Wednesday morning in North Carolina asked me what I was going to do, and I told him I was basically going through the same thing he was. I'm caught up in the flurry and flattery of being recruited and I've got to do what he has to do: Stand up for the right thing. And, I told him, that's what I was going to do.

Rick Telander of *Sports Illustrated* and the *Chicago Sun-Times* really has the ability to lock in on me, and he wrote an article in the *Sun-Times* that Mary read to me over the phone on Wednesday when I was recruiting in North Carolina. I don't know where he gets his insights, but I've come to really appreciate them. He has a tap into me as if he were a very close friend. His article was about why I would go to UCLA. He had gone over to the campus, and his reasoning fit like a glove. I told Mary, "Wow, this is right on." But there was one flaw. It only reflected a selfish viewpoint. It only accounted for, "What does Gary Barnett want?" It wasn't what was best for Gary Barnett's family, meaning all of the people who would be most affected by the decision.

I flew to Dayton later that day and President Bienen sent me a fax about a rumor that had been circulating. The rumor was that one of the glitches in our agreement was that Northwestern wasn't doing enough for the coaches. I don't know where that came from because I felt Northwestern had taken care of that and I never had a public—or private—comment disputing it.

Then Pat Ryan, the president of the board of trustees, called, and I vented some of my frustration to him. I talked to Jeff Genyk, who had enlisted the opinions of all the assistants, and it looked like all but two definitely wanted to stay. I called Mary and she was ambivalent about starting over.

And then I had a talk with myself.

In the next few weeks I was supposed to be accepting a number of coach of the year awards for what we had done at Northwestern—not what we had done at Georgia or Oklahoma or UCLA or anyplace else. How could I be at one of these banquets and be introduced as ... the UCLA coach?

Glen Mason had taken the job at Georgia—briefly—and it made me think, "How do you go in and tell your kids? What do you say to them? What do I tell these kids is the reason I'm going to UCLA? What's the reason I'd give them for going?" The only reasons I could give them would be that I like warm weather and I like to play golf, and those are pretty damned selfish.

We had become only the second school in history to beat Notre Dame, Michigan, and Penn State in the same season—Michigan State had done it twice, decades before—and if we had beaten USC in the Rose Bowl we would have become the first to beat all four.

I felt like I'd pushed, pulled, and thrown this thing to the top of the hill, but we weren't so solidly on the top that it couldn't roll right back down if I got off.

Not that I didn't trust Vandy with the job, because I absolutely would have. It was just that I didn't think I had quite seen it through. The program was so awful when I got here and I couldn't stomach the possibility of having it return to that and feeling responsible for it.

Maybe losing the Rose Bowl was part of this feeling. It didn't tarnish the season but it made me feel like we needed to come back and win it.

Most important, though, my first full-year's recruiting class was in its junior year. And I can distinctly remember sitting in

Jon Burns' home, and a couple of other kids' homes, and being asked if I was going to be there when they graduated. I said I would be.

You've got to say and mean those things as a coach at a struggling program because it is one of the strongest selling points you can make. Kids are looking for consistency and stability and so the stability I offered was that I was going to be here. That was the only stability that I could offer.

There were at least four other guys that I'd made this promise to and I couldn't walk out on that. I couldn't walk out on what had happened here.

Mary and I had made a conscious decision when we got into college coaching that if we had to make moves, we'd only make them if it was the best thing for our family. When we went from Durango to Boulder there was no question that the move was the best thing for the four of us. And when we moved from Boulder to Northwestern it was again the best thing for our family—which was still only four at that time.

Now our family had grown to 10 coaches, their wives, their children, plus 105 other guys. So my decisions affected more than just four people. If it were just me, personally, by myself, I probably would have gone to UCLA. But it wasn't just me, and so that reasoning wasn't important.

What's important is what you decide is going to drive your decisions. If you're going to have any integrity you must follow through on what you say. I teach a sport that is the epitome of team, and I ask my players to throw away selfishness. I must do the same.

I wasn't going to make my decision until Thursday but by Wednesday night my mind was made up. I called Peter Dalis at UCLA, and I said, "Peter, I want this job.... But I can't take it."

He said, "Nooo."

I said, "It's not the right thing for my family. I want you to know you guys have been unbelievable." They had been. They had done everything humanly possible. We discussed it for a while but he could tell I wasn't going to give in.

That was the hardest phone call I've ever had to make but I haven't looked back for a second. Then I called Rick Taylor and told him and I think he was genuinely surprised. I think a lot of people were.

This decision was not about money. If it was about money, I wouldn't be at Northwestern. But why should money be the ultimate gauge? We had achieved something no one thought possible and I thought I might be able to keep making a difference here that I might not be able to make somewhere else.

You only get a couple of times in your life to make a difference. You've just got to recognize when those times are.

The meaning of "Expect Victory" has now changed. And now we might be able to sell our guys on "Belief *With* Evidence." I heard one of the guys say they think we'll change the motto to "Demand Victory." I don't think so, though.

If we wanted to feel a sense of being burdened by what we've accomplished I suppose we could. But, really, the challenge is just as it's always been.

The simple things have to be done again. You don't necessarily build directly from one year to the next because each year and each team has its own distinct set of problems—or opportunities, as the case may be. You have to identify the essence of each team. The decisions that have to be made, the circumstances that have to be considered, are different every year.

But what must remain the same is the conviction, the faith, the belief, the trust. Drawing on these core qualities, that's the continuity. And you've got to keep making those decisions with the same humbleness and hunger.

We went into 1995 without any evidence that we could reach the Rose Bowl. Now we have evidence. That hill's been covered. We've gone up and reached the summit. But when you get to the top of one hill, what you discover is that it's not just one peak and then a valley. It's a mountain range, and there are just more peaks out there—all higher than the one you just climbed.

That doesn't mean you have to go all the way back down to sea level to scale the others. You can use the ridges and the heights that you've already attained, even if sometimes you step down a little as you climb back up.

For our first spring meeting in 1996, we made up placards for every player who had received any sort of award last season. We had an ovation for each guy and I said, "Men, that was a heck of a job."

I had a placard, too. Then I said, "1995's over," and I put my placard in a trash can marked "1995." One by one, our players did, too.

Appendix

The 1992 text of thoughts on the "servant leader," as compiled and written by Robert P. Neuschel of the Kellogg Graduate School of Management, and adapted by Gary Barnett for weekly discussion with his seniors.

Week One:

1. It is not the lot of the leader to be served but rather his/her privilege to serve. "Ich Dien" appears prominently on the crest of the Prince of Wales. It says so simply, "I Serve." Putting that concept into practice is the basis for developing the servant leader concept.

2. Efforts to gain human understanding should dominate a leader's thinking and actions. The leader is neither a statistician nor an engineer but rather is a leader of human beings in a world of Homo sapiens.

3. The leader needs the capacity to meet adversity without succumbing to emotional paralysis or withdrawal and without lashing out at colleagues or subordinates. One significant test of quality leadership is how well the leader copes with disappointments, defeat, or some form of overriding adversity. Voltaire, in praising this quality in the Duke of Marlborough, called it, "Calm courage in the midst of tumult, that serenity of soul in danger, which is the greatest gift of nature for command."

Week Two:

1. Stamina is the leader's ultimate resource. Little is much good without endurance. This is evidenced by the ability to work long and hard, especially under pressure or after disappointment. I re-

197

call a corporate president recently saying, "My greatest strength grows out of my tenacity." Life and leadership both are more of a marathon than a dash.

2. No amount of technique can produce courage. Courage comes from the heart, and the soul, and it can hardly be intellectualized.

3. Success in interpersonal relations does not depend on intellectual endowment; it depends rather on basic intelligence and emotional maturity....

Week Three:

1. All effective leaders have a deep and abiding want for accomplishment that glues together other important attributes such as:
—human understanding
—integrity
—total sense of responsibility
—touch of wisdom
—capacity to be big
—decisiveness
—courage

2. The high performing leader must have and display (and be perceived to have) an unswerving sense of moral decency.

3. The head is smart but not always wise. Perhaps the highest art in leadership is to balance the head and the heart. The effective leader must have both head and heart. Each situation requires a different balance of the two. There is no formula or scientific way to determine what this balance should be. This is part of the reason why being a talented leader is more art than science.

Week Four:

1. The capacity to quickly assess that which is important is a quality common to most successful executives. Some call this an instinct for the essential. This is really basic to solid, common sense, an invaluable asset to an effective manager/leader.

2. The image of the leader is not his superficial self but rather

the sum total of a system of values demonstrated over time. When this manifestation is clear and consistent and reflects a quality of personal integrity, it is a powerful instrument. Integrity implies that a person has developed over time a consistent ordering of his system of values, attitudes and goals.

3. The effective leader is mentally and emotionally grown up. He has matured—is objective and thoughtful. Such a leader must be free of arrogance and moodiness and realistically well-adjusted to life.

Week Five:

1. The leader needs vast amounts of physical, spiritual and psychic energy. Frustrations, disappointments and "high mountains" will drain energy. The pressure to compete, to make changes, to face the new demands will be physically and emotionally tiring—it will be energy draining and there is a need to continually replenish the leader's sources of energy.

2. The leader must have a high tolerance for ambiguity and learn to live and be productive in an increasingly uncertain environment. The managerial playing field will be messy and require a great deal of sorting out and striving to operate on an even keel in an ever-changing and churning sea.

3. The leader needs unswerving strength of character. The choices will be difficult. The temptations many. Making the right decisions will not be so much intellectual as demanding of one's character.

Week Six:

1. The effective leader energizes people as he/she leads them. Above that the leader needs the passion to inspire.

2. The leader must have the courage, the inner peace of mind and soul and the willpower to take difficult and sometimes very lonely positions.

3. Margaret Thatcher in her remarkable career demonstrated many virtues. Foremost among them were: constancy (she is predictable), determination, decisiveness and sheer grit.

Week Seven:

1. The leader needs much more than integrity to be successful. But without integrity and trust nothing else matters much. In fact, integrity and trust are the foundation stones of all voluntary leadership.

2. The leader needs special wisdom and courage to sort out conflicting demands and desires—e.g., production vs. humanity, output vs. environment, sales vs. production, short-term vs. long-term.... The tough parts of leadership are the choices that must be made.

3. Remember that leadership and followership represent a continuum. Followership sets the pattern for leadership. The leader can not cheat up and get trust from below. The leader's own style of followership provides the model for his/her own people to imitate.

Week Eight:

1. Most people desire to be led. They usually want to be part of a going thing. We are a society of organizations. We want to belong. But people want a firm sense of direction from the leader. The trumpet sound must be clear.

2. The leader must be an extraordinary agent for change. In this world of rapid change and discontinuities, the leader must be out front to encourage change and growth and to show the way to bring it about. There are two important requisites to bringing about change:

    A. Knowing the technical requirements of the change.
    B. Understanding the attitudinal and motivational demands
       to bringing it about.

Both requisites are critically necessary. But more often than not, failure to change will result from inadequate or inappropriate motivation—not from lack of technical smarts.

3. Many great military commanders were as natural as children—straightforward—not artful—no acting—no pretense. Naturalness is a priceless virtue in leadership.

Week Nine:

1. The effective manager/leader must have a capacity for abstraction, vision and the ability to conceptualize. The leader must have great facility to translate the conceptual into concrete specifics that are readily understood and meaningful to the people in the organization. This is translating vision into reality.

2. There is a strong need for commitment and not just compliance. All high-performing organizations have key leaders and sub-leaders imbued with deep commitment.

3. The effective leader is constantly inspirationally dissatisfied. It is a healthy kind of dissatisfaction that encourages persevering through daily challenges and trials and always reaching for higher levels of performance.

Week Ten:

1. The mature manager/leader needs:
—a high flashpoint
—a soft but strong voice
—deep reserves of energy
—an inner peace—an internal calmness that fosters stability in the face of tumult
—unswerving strength of character
—a well-managed ego
—a lot of smarts and still growing

2. You have to be able to say "yes" or "no" crisply. Don't waffle. You can withhold a decision but do not be or appear to be tentative in the process.

3. In the National Football League, they still want to know how fast a player runs the 40-yard dash or the number of tackles made per game. But increasingly more attention is being devoted to a player's values, habits, personality and ethics. There is a strong message here as we evaluate the qualities of leaders. While both skill and character are vital, increasingly character will dominate.

Northwestern 1996 Rose Bowl Roster

No.	Name	Pos.	Class	Hometown
48	Allen, Eugene	DB	So.	Indianapolis, IN
32	Autry, Adrian	RB	So.	Long Grove, IL
24	Autry, Darnell	RB	So.	Tempe, AZ
17	Barnes, Josh	DB	So.	Aurora, CO
5	Bates, D'Wayne	WR	So.	Aiken, SC
86	Beazley, Dave	WR	Sr.	Crystal Lake, IL
20	Bennett, William	FS	Sr.	Tempe, AZ
34	Brown, Levelle	RB	Fr.	Naperville, IL
71	Brownstein, Bo	OL	Fr.	Englewood, CO
12	Broxterman, Mark	QB	Fr.	Homewood, IL
49	Buck, Kevin	OLB	Fr.	Miami, FL
80	Burden, John	WR	So.	Orlando, FL
81	Burns, Jon	DT	So.	Kankakee, IL
7	Burrell, Aaron	RB	Fr.	Cedar Rapids, IA
14	Burton, Paul	P	Sr.	Framingham, MA
47	Campbell, Morgan	CB	Fr.	Ontario, Canada
61	Chabot, Justin	OT	Sr.	Oxford, OH
33	Collier, Eric	SS	Jr.	Dixon, IL
11	Conoway, Gerald	DB	Fr.	Detroit, MI
89	Curry, Larry	DT	Sr.	Granite City, IL
36	Dailey, Casey	OLB	Jr.	La Verne, CA
2	Davis, Mike	WR	Fr.	San Diego, CA
76	Dodge, Tony	OL	Fr.	McHenry, IL
83	Drexler, Darren	TE	Sr.	Kirkwood, MO
88	DuBose, KeJaun	DT	Jr.	Jennings, MO
65	Dyra, Jeff	DL	Fr.	Chicago, IL
51	Fitzgerald, Pat	ILB	Jr.	Orland Park, IL
35	Fordenwalt, Matt	TE	Fr.	Seville, OH
99	Friedrich, Ryan	DL	Fr.	Stevens Point, WI
55	Gardner, Barry	LB	So.	Harvey, IL
43	Gaston, Stafford	LB	Fr.	Oklahoma City, OK
92	Giometti, Mike	DL	Sr.	Lake Forest, IL
66	Gnos, Graham	OL	Sr.	Bloomington, MN
38	Gooch, Tyrone	RB	Fr.	Bolingbrook, IL
13	Gowins, Brian	PK	So.	Birmingham, AL
84	Graham, Shane	TE	Sr.	Thousand Oaks, CA
1	Guess, Larry	DB	Jr.	Hinsdale, IL
4	Hamdorf, Chris	QB	Jr.	Iowa City, IA
85	Harpring, Brian	TE	Sr. (5)	Dunwoody, GA
46	Hartl, Matt	FB	So.	Denver, CO
70	Hemmerle, Brian	OT	Fr.	Louisville, KY
41	Henkelmann, Matt	WR	So.	Linton, ND
53	Holmes, Don	LB	So.	South Holland, IL
8	Hughes, Tim	QB	Jr.	Gridley, CA
3	Ismaeli, Hudhaifa	DB	Jr.	Pittsburgh, PA
74	Janus, Paul	OL	Jr.	Edgerton, WI
57	Johnson, Rob	C	Sr. (5)	Chicago, IL
39	Jones, Shannon	PK	So.	Grand Rapids, MI

203

No.	Name	Pos.	Class	Hometown
78	Kardos, Brian	OT	Sr.	Springfield, IL
40	Kolar, Josh	LB	Fr.	Wilmette, IL
79	LaBelle, Bryan	OT	So.	Kent, WA
91	Lapadula, Marc	LB	Fr.	Allentown, PA
37	Leary, Faraji	RB	So.	Buffalo Grove, IL
69	Leeder, Chris	OL	So.	Rockford, MI
44	Lozowski, Keith	OLB	Jr.	Palatine, IL
16	Martin, Chris	CB	Sr.	Tampa, FL
58	Matiyow, Jason	C	Fr.	Council Bluffs, IA
88	McCaffrey, James	TE	Fr.	Schaumburg, IL
45	McGrew, Mike	FB	Sr.	Chicago Heights, IL
89	McLain, Randy	OLB	Fr.	Isanti, MN
42	Morrison, Tucker	LB	Jr.	Port Orchard, WA
22	Musso, Brian	WR	Jr.	Hinsdale, IL
23	Musso, Scott	RB	Jr.	Hinsdale, IL
26	Nelson, Jr., Mike	DB	So.	Plano, TX
54	Offenbacher, Shawn	OL	So.	Chesterfield, MO
75	Padgett, Ryan	OG	Sr.	Bellevue, WA
72	Peterson, Kevin	OG	Sr.	Lockport, IL
77	Pugh, Chad	OG	Sr.	Oswego, IL
15	Ray, Rodney	CB	Sr. (5)	Ferguson, MO
94	Reiff, Joe	DT	Sr.	Cedar Rapids, IA
95	Rice, Matt	DT	Jr.	Middleton, WI
96	Robey, Ray	DT	Jr.	Rockford, IL
29	Rooney, Chris	CB	Sr.	Minneapolis, MN
59	Ross, Jason	LB	So.	Dayton, OH
19	Rubin, Brian	DB	Fr.	Detroit, MI
98	Russ, Bobby	DL	So.	Calumet City, IL
31	Sanders, Kyle	OLB	Fr.	Jackson, MI
52	Scharf, Tim	ILB	Jr.	Rockford, IL
90	Schmidt, Thor	OLB	So.	Santa Barbara, CA
10	Schnur, Steve	QB	Sr.	St. Louis, MO
47	Shein, Geoff	OLB	Sr. (5)	Glencoe, IL
56	Sidwell, Zach	OLB	Fr.	Kearney, NB
82	Steele, Hasani	WR	Fr.	Glen Ellyn, IL
30	Stewart, Matt	FS	Jr.	Omaha, NB
63	Strikwerda, Nathan	OL	Jr.	Madison, WI
87	Stuart, Joel	TE	So.	Elyria, OH
50	Sutter, Danny	ILB	Sr.	Peoria, IL
25	Swenson, Jeff	WR	So.	Spencer, IA
97	Taylor, Gladston	DL	Fr.	Missouri City, TX
28	Tomes, Shawn	RB	Fr.	San Antonio, TX
73	Tomkiel, Mark	OT	So.	Chicago, IL
27	Valenzisi, Sam	PK	Sr. (5)	Westlake, OH
93	Walker, Jason	TE	Jr.	Cincinnati, OH
68	Warren, Mike	OLB	Sr. (5)	Antioch, IL
18	Waterman, Toussaint	WR	Jr.	Pontiac, MI
60	Wendland, Jason	OT	Sr.	Simi Valley, CA
21	Wilkerson, Fred	DB	So.	Detroit, MI
64	Yeager, Larry	OL	Fr.	Troy, MI

Index

205

Index

Index

210